# Brian Howe

# Portfolio

## Case Studies for Business English

Longman

To the memory of my father,
CLIFF HOWE,
for whom business was not
so much about position or
remuneration as about
doing things well.

**Longman Group UK Limited**
*Longman House, Burnt Mill, Harlow,*
*Essex CM20 2JE, England*
*and Associated Companies throughout the world.*

© Longman Group Limited 1987

First published 1987
Sixth impression 1994

ISBN 0-582-85246-3

Set in 'Monophoto' Rockwell and Helvetica
Produced by Longman Singapore Publishers Pte Ltd
Printed in Singapore

Designed by Robert Wheeler
Illustrated by Jerry Collins

**Author's acknowledgements**

The author would like to thank all those who have contributed ideas and suggestions to this book. In particular, he would like to thank Alan Harding and his colleagues at Sundridge Park for their validation work, Oxfam for their help with Unit 8, *Oxfam* and Ivor Campbell for the idea behind Unit 9, *A severe case of TSV*. Very special thanks are due to Jane Howe for her rigorous critique of the original material and her unfailing encouragement during the project.

**Acknowledgements**

We are grateful to the following for permission to reproduce copyright material:

International Management for extracts from *International Management* Copyright © McGraw-Hill Publications Co. All rights reserved; Joint Industry Committee for National Readership Surveys for data from *National Readership Survey* (JICNARS) Jan–Dec 1985; the author, Professor Karl Wieck for an extract from his article 'The Management of Organizational Change Among Loosely Coupled Elements' from pp 3–4 *In Search of Excellence* (pub Harper & Row); John Adair whose 'The Mast Contract' was adapted for 'The Tower.'

We are grateful to the following for permission to reproduce copyright photographs:

Ace Photo Agency for pages 31 (left) and 33 (bottom); Aspect Picture Library Limited for page 26; Art Directors Photo Library for page 34 (bottom); Richard Bird for page 34 (top); Canadian Pacific Rail for page 2; John Cleare/Mountain Camera for page 8; Colorific Photo Library Limited for page 59 (background); Daily Express for page 22 (middle) (photo by Longman photo unit); The Daily Telegraph for page 22 (middle top) (photo by Longman photo unit); ELE International Limited for page 11 (background); Ford Motor Company for page 50; The Guardian for page 22 (middle bottom) (photo by Longman photo unit); The Image Bank for page 33 (top); Longman photo unit for pages 1 (left and right), 3 (background), 5, 7, 10, 14, 17, 19, 21 (background), 24, 52 and 64; William MacQuitty for page 31 (right); Network Photographers for page 37; The Picture Library for page 65 (Rob Stratton); The Sun for page 22 (bottom) (photo by Longman photo unit); Times Newspapers Limited for page 22 (top) (photo by Longman photo unit); Uniphoto Picture Agency (DD Emmrich) for page 68; Zefa Picture Library (UK) Limited for page 1 (Clive Sawyer).

Cover photographs by Image Bank (photo by B. Rokeach) (top), NAAS Picture Library (bottom).

# Introduction

*P*ORTFOLIO is a collection of business case studies and activities for use during a business English course. It is designed to develop the communication skills of course participants at an intermediate level and above who are experienced managers or students of business studies.

Each unit of *Portfolio* consists of an open-ended business problem which students must firstly analyze and then solve. The problems in each unit are presented through sequences of realistic documents and diagrams with a minimum of linking narrative text. The student therefore has to assimilate information in the forms which they will normally receive it in the real world.

## The contents

*Portfolio* consists of 15 major units in which different business related problems are presented to students for solution. The units vary in length, subject matter and exploitation techniques but all are designed to encourage students to take part in lively discussions or role plays in which they can practise newly acquired language and skills.

Between the main units there are six sub-units called *Pause for Thought*. These are short fillers designed as springboards for business discussions.

To prepare students for taking part in the discussions and role plays deriving from each unit, the book begins with a reference unit in which the appropriate language is set out in an easily accessible form.

The accompanying audio cassette contains the dialogues incorporated in the majority of the units.

## To the student

The aim of this book is to help you to take part in realistic business situations in English. Each unit is a business story which you must help to finish. The situations are presented through realistic business documents such as letters, diagrams and memos. You will handle these as you would handle documents in real life. As you discuss them with your colleagues, you will begin to understand the business problem facing you. You will then discuss these problems and work out with your colleagues the best solution. In each unit you will do the talking. Your teacher will help you with language points where necessary. The main aim, however, is for you to communicate successfully even if you do make some mistakes in the language you use. Your teacher will deal with these after each case.

## To the course organizer

In general terms the main units lend themselves to one of two main exploitation techniques:

**1 The Case Study Approach** (Students as outsiders): In this approach the students will proceed as a group through the exhibits analyzing the situation and identifying the problems. Once the case has been clearly assimilated, students can take part in a round table discussion with a view to presenting possible solutions and finally agreeing on one of them.

**2 The Simulation Approach** (Students as insiders): In this approach students may adopt specific roles or responsibilities either as they proceed through the body of the case or once they have assimilated the whole case as a group.

Specific suggestions for both the above approaches can be found in the accompanying *Teacher's Guide.*

# Contents

# Language reference unit

In this unit you will find some of the typical language used in standard business situations. Since each of the cases and simulations in the main part of this book will require you to take part in such typical situations, it is best that you practise some of the phrases and gambits used in these situations first. You may also like to keep the relevant page of this unit open while you take part in the cases and simulations. This unit is divided into the following sections:

1 Information presentation
2 Negotiations
3 Meetings
4 Product and service presentation

## 1 Information presentation

**Introducing the exhibit**
I'd like to show you this graph.
Have a look at this diagram.
I think this bar chart will be of interest to you.

**Labelling the exhibit**
It's a graph showing the seasonal sales of . . .
It's an advertisement for . . .
It's an organization chart of . . .
It's a telex from . . .

**Describing the structure of the exhibit**
The horizontal axis shows . . .
The vertical axis represents . . .
The curve shows . . .

**Describing the main features of the exhibit**
You will see immediately that . . .
Its most significant feature is . . .
A very interesting point is . . .

**Interpreting an exhibit:**
This seems to suggest that . . .
In my opinion this means that . . .
This implies that . . .
It is quite clear that . . .

**Presenting opinions**
My view is that . . .
I think that . . .
My opinion is that . . .

**Making recommendations**
I think we should . . .
I feel we ought to . . .
I suggest that we . . .
I recommend that . . .

**Describing the content of an exhibit**

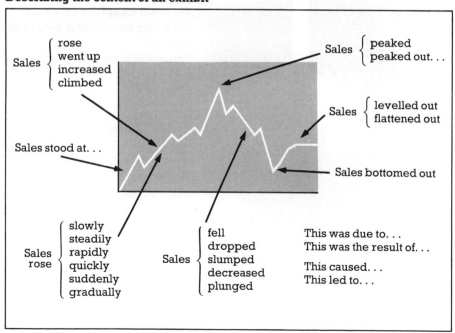

Sales { rose / went up / increased / climbed

Sales { peaked / peaked out. . .

Sales { levelled out / flattened out

Sales stood at. . .

Sales bottomed out

Sales rose { slowly / steadily / rapidly / quickly / suddenly / gradually

Sales { fell / dropped / slumped / decreased / plunged

This was due to. . .
This was the result of. . .

This caused. . .
This led to. . .

# 2 Negotiations

### Agreeing a procedure

I think we should first of all establish a procedure.

May I suggest that we begin by . . .?

After that . . ./ Finally . . .

That's OK. with us.

Fine.

### Opening the negotiations

Can we begin by outlining our view of the situation?

Our position is this.

What we are looking for is . . .

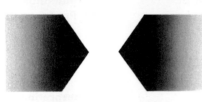

Our position is quite clear. Firstly, . . .

Our main worry is . . .

We hope to achieve . . .

### Exploring positions

How important is . . .

Supposing we were to say . . .?

Can we clarify . . .?

This is the most important factor from our point of view.

How would you feel if . . .?

### Establishing the bargaining zone

There is no problem as far as . . . is concerned.

We could not accept . . .

That would be out of the question.

Let's take a purely hypothetical situation.

The main problem here is . . .

Suppose that we . . .?

Would you be willing to . . .?

We have no room for manoeuvre here.

### Bargaining

We can offer . . .

We could not go beyond . . .

We would be willing to . . .

This is our final offer.

What would you say if . . .?

Our proposal would be . . .

Our bottom line is . . .

We could accept this only if . . .

We would have to refer back on this one.

This would present real problems for us.

### Settling

I think we're within reach of an agreement here.

The last sticking point is . . .

We can accept that.

It's a deal then.

There are a few loose ends we'd like to tie up.

If you can see your way to . . .

That would be acceptable to us.

I think we have an agreement.

# 3 Meetings

### Opening the meeting

- Right. Can we start please?
- O.K. Let's kick off. . .
- Shall we begin

**Content, flow and direction of meeting**

### Establishing targets

- The main aim of this meeting is to. . .
- The first thing we must do is. . .

**Targets**

### Establishing targets

- I think we should first of all look at. . .
- Finally we should try to. . .

### Asking for initial contributions

- Could you kick off, James, with. . .?
- I'd like you to start, John, with. . .

**Initial contributions**

### Asking for initial contributions

- Perhaps you could start, John. . .
- Would you like to begin, Sue, with your. . .?

### Agreeing

- I agree.
- We accept that.
- You're right.

**Main discussion**

### Asking for opinions

- What do you think, Jim?
- What's your opinion, Margaret?
- What's the view of the sales department, Jack?

### Disagreeing

- I disagree.
- I don't think it will work.

### Asking for opinions

- How do you feel about Jack's idea, John?
- What's your reaction to Sue's suggestion?

### Dealing with interruptions

- Just a minute. Let me finish.
- Hang on. . . I haven't finished.

### Interrupting

- Can I come in here?
- Could I say something?
- Just a minute!

### Slowing down a meeting

- Just a moment. I think we should look at this more carefully.

### Speeding up a meeting

- Time is short. Can we move on to. . .?
- Can we leave that till later and go on to. . .?

### Dealing with digressions

- I think we're getting away from the subject
- Can we get back to the main problem?

### Digressing

- Can I digress for a moment?
- I think we should look in passing at. . .

### Bringing a meeting to its targets

- Right. Let's see what we've got.

**Decisions**

### Bringing a meeting to its targets

- OK. Can we come to a decision on this?

### Summarising and concluding

- OK. Let's recap. . .

### Summarising and concluding

- Right. We have decided then to. . .

### Closing the meeting

- Let's finish there.

### Closing the meeting

- OK. Let's call it a day.

# 4 Product and service presentation

**Describing the features and benefits of a product**

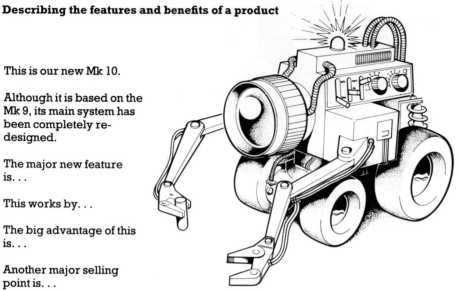

This is our new Mk 10.

Although it is based on the Mk 9, its main system has been completely re-designed.

The major new feature is. . .

This works by. . .

The big advantage of this is. . .

Another major selling point is. . .

The major difference between this and the Mk 9 is. . .

One interesting new feature is. . .

Another improvement we have built in is. . .

This device here is for. . .

The major benefits of the Mk 10 can be summed up as. . .

**Comparing competitive products**

The Mk 10
{
has the edge on . . .
compares well with . . .
performs better than . . .
is ahead of . . .
is far ahead of . . .
is superior to . . .
is far superior to . . .
}
the Mk 9.

# Airline

## Bottoms on seats

**UNIT 1**

A Canadian airline loses some important customers, invents a new slogan and attempts a comeback.

The problem facing Jacques Rousseau, President of InterAir, was simple to describe but a little more difficult to solve. In order to maximize revenues on its Toronto-Montreal commuter route, the airline needed business passengers willing to pay the top fare of $130 return. But to attract business passengers InterAir had to offer more frequent flights. Extra flights, however, created extra capacity which could not be filled by the available business market. This then was the problem that now faced Rousseau. A year after the start of the new flights his message to the InterAir planning staff was brief and to the point. 'We are an airline, ladies and gentlemen, not furniture removers . . . I want bottoms on those empty seats FAST!' Six weeks later InterAir announced a new deal for travellers on the Toronto route.

1 Study InterAir's latest advertisement below.

2 What is its main selling point on the Toronto-Montreal route?

3 What 'frills' does it offer to the business traveller?

4 What is the new deal for the non-business passenger?

1 Listen to InterAir's recorded information service.

2 Write down the prices of each type of ticket.

3 Write down the booking conditions for each ticket.

---

# The fastest way to business *and pleasure* in Toronto

You have a 7 a.m. telephone call from the Toronto Office. They want you there YESTERDAY. What do you do? You phone InterAir of course. No we can't perform miracles but we can GUARANTEE you a seat on our next flight to Toronto. (And there are 9 flights daily!) On the way we'll provide you with free drinks, breakfast and your morning newspaper so that by 10.30 you can be downtown in Big T, relaxed and prepared for a full day's work. And by the way, do you know that with InterAir's new, low price, reserve-ahead fares your wife and friends can now accompany you for a day's shopping for as little as $40 round trip? Ring us now for details.

Call us on 434 4000

# A customer complains and the competition responds

Six months later the InterAir planning staff had reason to be pleased. Load factors on the Toronto-Montreal route were soaring and total revenue or yields were rising too. The only cloud on the horizon was a new advertising campaign by a rather old fashioned competitor but this was not considered important until a member of staff overheard a conversation at Toronto airport. It was shortly after this that the first dip in the revenue curve was picked up by InterAir's route analysis computer.

1 Listen to the conversation overheard at Toronto airport.

2 List the problems encountered by the InterAir business passenger.

3 What solution does his colleague suggest?

1 Study the advertisement that appeared in the Montreal Courier.

2 List the advantages of travelling to Toronto by rail.

3 Suggest reasons why InterAir's load factors are rising while its revenues are falling.

# Six ways to improve an airline

1 Introduce panoramic windows so that your passengers can enjoy the countryside as they travel.

2 Provide your passengers with their own hostess to give them the attention they would expect from a First Class service.

3 Introduce truly reclining seats that will not upset the passenger behind.

4 Widen your seats and double the leg room available.

5 Knock $50 off the round trip price.

6 Give your passengers their own desk.

On TransCanadian Rail we treat our Business passengers as they would treat their own customers. For comfort, service and economy there is nothing like it. Our Montreal-Toronto Business Express leaves Montreal at 7.15 every morning and arrives in Toronto at 10.30. You don't need to make a reservation. Just pay on the train. Why pay sky-high fares when you can travel in comfort for only $80 round trip?

***TransCanadian Rail – the best way to business in Toronto***

# InterAir changes course
# A new image, a new slogan

The following month's revenue figures confirmed Rousseau's suspicions. Although load factors were now at a record level, revenues were falling dramatically. This pointed to only one conclusion. The airline's premium passengers were transferring to other forms of transport and InterAir was fast becoming the preferred form of travel for the bargain hunters of Toronto and Montreal. Two days before a meeting called to analyze the latest situation, Jacques Rousseau circulated a memo to his planning staff. It contained not only the information below but also Rousseau's own suggestion for the central thrust of a new sales campaign to win back the airline's business clientele. Scrawled across the top of the memo in Rousseau's handwriting were the words, 'InterAir: The Business Person's Airline.'

 With the new slogan in mind, divide into 3 groups to study the available information. Each group should interpret one of the diagrams for the whole group.

1 Describe the changing pattern of business travel between the two cities.

2 Who are the winners and who are the losers?

1 Analyze and compare the time components of travel between the two cities.

2 What are the strengths and weaknesses of each form of travel?

---

**Montreal-Toronto route analysis this year**
(daily business journeys)
last year's percentages in brackets

- 60% road (65%)
- 30% rail (20%)
- 10% air (15%)

Total number of daily business journeys 3500
Distance Montreal-Toronto 330 miles

1 Describe the changes in InterAir's fare structure.

2 Who has benefited from the changes?

---

**Comparative breakdown of journey times Montreal-Toronto**

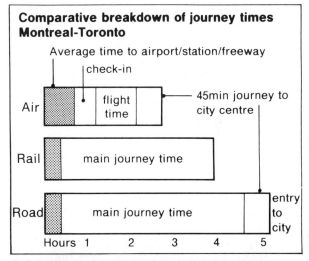

Average time to airport/station/freeway

check-in

Air — flight time — 45min journey to city centre

Rail — main journey time

Road — main journey time — entry to city

Hours 1 2 3 4 5

3 Calculate and compare the average revenues for both years.

---

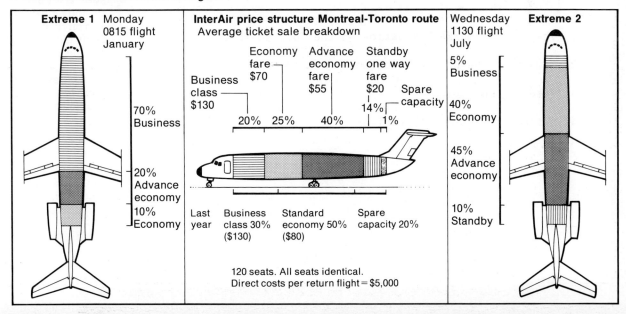

**Extreme 1** Monday 0815 flight January

- 70% Business
- 20% Advance economy
- 10% Economy

**InterAir price structure Montreal-Toronto route**
Average ticket sale breakdown

Business class $130 — 20%
Economy fare $70 — 25%
Advance economy fare $55 — 40%
Standby one way fare $20 — 14%
Spare capacity — 1%

| Last year | Business class 30% ($130) | Standard economy 50% ($80) | Spare capacity 20% |

120 seats. All seats identical.
Direct costs per return flight = $5,000

**Extreme 2** Wednesday 1130 flight July

- 5% Business
- 40% Economy
- 45% Advance economy
- 10% Standby

# Getting to the bottom of things

Rousseau's memo and the latest information from the market place concentrated the minds of InterAir's planning staff. Over the next few days various informal discussions took place. The following are some of the views expressed.

> The problem as I see it is that we've simply got to separate the business passenger from the discount passenger. What about a curtain that you can move according to the flight's booking pattern?

> Let's face the facts. The average business bottom is larger than the average non-business bottom. We've got to convert a proportion of our seats to the wider executive type. The question is what proportion?

> I think we're just tinkering with the problem. In my view we should convert the whole aircraft to wider seats, raise service standards, raise the price and start a massive advertising campaign around a frequent traveller offer. What about offering one free ticket for every ten Business tickets bought from InterAir? That'll bring our premium customers back . . .

> In my view it's nothing to do with the seats themselves. It's to do with allocating enough business seats to meet the expected demand for any one flight. We've got a computer. Make it predict the demand patterns and block off the seats accordingly . . .

> We must not forget the importance of ground facilities. You've got to pamper the business person. Give them a separate lounge, priority check-in desks and special service on board and they'll be happy . . .

```
InterAir Planning Group Meeting

A G E N D A

1  The present market situation on the Toronto-Montreal route

2  Causes of the present problem

3  InterAir objectives

4  Methods to achieve objectives:
   a) Price structure
   b) Reservation systems
   c) In-flight seating/service/organization
   d) Ground service
   e) Advertising

5  Plan of action
```

The next day the agenda for the strategy meeting was circulated. Study the headings and then hold a meeting to work out the best way to solve InterAir's problems.

# Safety first

A construction company tries to improve its safety record.

There's enough spilled blood and broken bones in our accident log book to write a thriller, Harry.

This is the construction industry, Bob. What do you expect?

This is A and G Construction. We set the standards for building in this country. Why aren't we doing the same for safety?

When Bob Anderson, Chairman of A and G Construction, got a bee in his bonnet, there had to be action. A and G has 150 construction sites around the country employing 8,000 men. Within a week each site manager had received a detailed questionnaire concerning the site's safety record. Three weeks after his brief but pointed conversation with Anderson, Harry Evans, A and G's Director of Personnel, had enough facts to go back to Anderson with an initial analysis of the problem.

1  Study the graph below.

2  Make a list of the main accident peaks.

3  Make a list of the accident troughs.

4  Describe any pattern you can see in A and G's daily accident record.

## A&G Construction Ltd
### Reported accidents by quarter hours of working day  (6 month average)

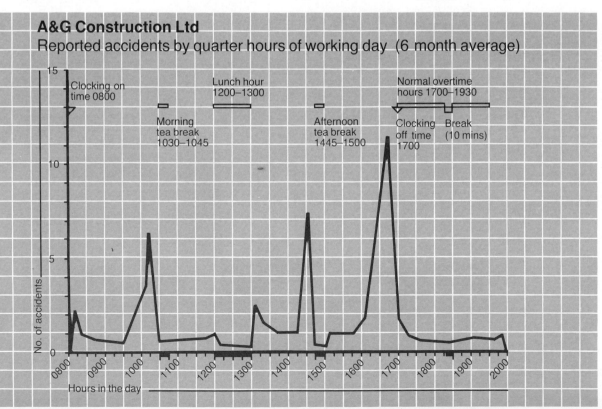

Clocking on time 0800

Morning tea break 1030–1045

Lunch hour 1200–1300

Afternoon tea break 1445–1500

Normal overtime hours 1700–1930

Clocking off time 1700

Break (10 mins)

No. of accidents

Hours in the day

# Some educated guesses

It took Bob Anderson only seconds to digest the graph. 'OK. So we now have a good overall picture, Harry. There's clearly a distinct pattern emerging here. The mornings are what I'd expect, but what the hell's happening in the afternoons?' He paused for a moment and then looked at the graph again. 'And you can't tell me it's because they're tired after lunch. Just look at the figures for over-time. It's the safest time in the whole day!' Harry Evans knew that Anderson loved a good graph. Now was the time to show him his pièce de résistance.

1 Study the breakdown of accident causes that Evans showed Anderson.

2 Explain in your own words the four different kinds of causes.

3 Identify the most common cause of accidents at A and G.

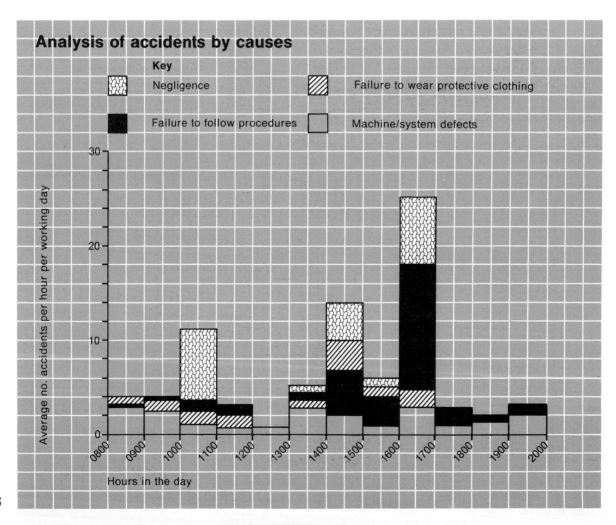

# From the horse's mouth

'Very nice Harry. I'm impressed. It's surprising what one man can do from an office. The trouble is though that we still don't know WHY these accidents are happening. Graphs are all very well but they're no substitute for the real thing. Now Harry, I want you to go out and get your shoes dirty. Visit some of the sites and talk to the guys who were injured. In the end the only way to find out what's happening is from the horse's mouth . . .'

A week later Harry Evans was once again facing Bob Anderson across the table in the A and G boardroom. The agenda for the meeting was summed up in a single sentence: 'Ways and means of reducing the incidence of accidents throughout A and G's U.K. sites.' Evans's personal notes, however, were more detailed. After all, Anderson would want more than a couple of graphs and a pair of muddy boots to show for his four weeks on the project so far.

1 Listen to three of the interviews Harry Evans had on the sites.

2 For each interview identify the injury that the person suffered.

3 For each interview identify a) the immediate and b) the longer term causes of the accident.

1 Study Evans's notes.

2 Decide how each item in the notes connects to the safety problems of A and G Industries.

3 Devise a series of recommendations for each of the items with the aim of reducing A and G's accident record.

*Safety meeting: 20/10 — NOTES*

*1 Work organisation on site: starting, finishing and break times and timing.*

*2 Maintenance. Shifts.*

*3 Supervision*

*4 Safety awareness: rules, procedures, warnings, publicity, training, sanctions, etc.*

*5 General working environment and conditions. Psychological factors, etc.*

# A tale of two Everests

## 1 The mountain

Mount Everest is the highest mountain in the world. Its peak at 8,846 metres has been climbed many times since the first successful expedition in 1953. Until 1975, however, no one had reached the peak via the notorious South West face. To Chris Bonington, one of the world's leading mountaineers, this route to the top of the world's highest mountain was one of the last great challenges in mountaineering.

### Bonington accepts the challenge.

Bonington knew that individual mountaineering skills alone would not be enough to conquer the mountain by this route. As there was only a small *weather window* open to him in any year, he had to move men and equipment quickly and efficiently up the mountain. To do this he needed a large expedition team with many different skills. The organization of such a team was the first major problem he had to face.

1 Study the organization chart below.

2 Make a list of the possible functions for each group.

3 Predict some of the problems that might exist within and between the various groups.

UNIT 3

Can a manufacturer of pumps learn anything from a famous mountaineer?

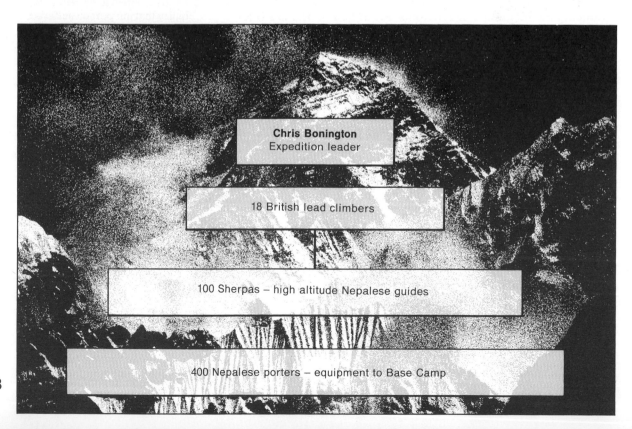

Chris Bonington
Expedition leader

18 British lead climbers

100 Sherpas – high altitude Nepalese guides

400 Nepalese porters – equipment to Base Camp

# Bonington's plan

1 Study Bonington's plan for the expedition below.

2 Listen to the account of each stage of the climb.

3 List the problems he had to face at each stage.

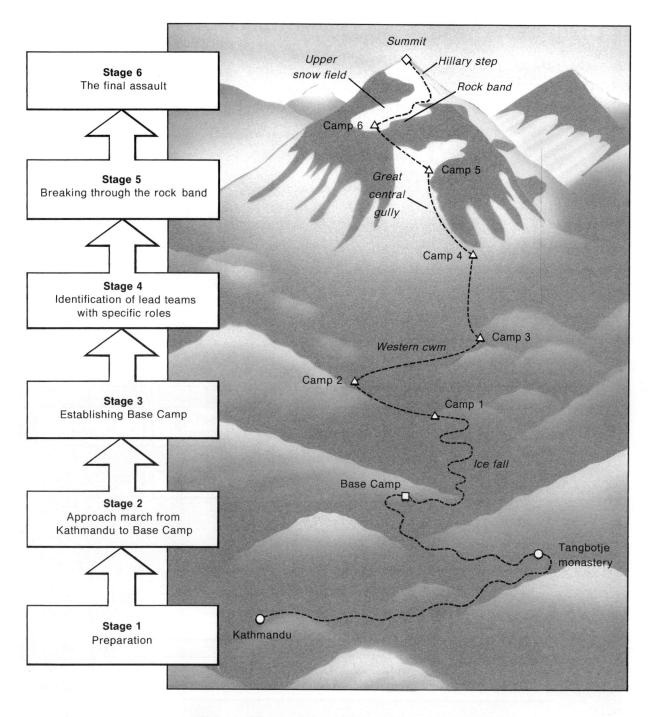

Stage 6
The final assault

Stage 5
Breaking through the rock band

Stage 4
Identification of lead teams
with specific roles

Stage 3
Establishing Base Camp

Stage 2
Approach march from
Kathmandu to Base Camp

Stage 1
Preparation

Summit

Upper
snow field
Hillary step

Rock band

Camp 6

Great
central
gully
Camp 5

Camp 4

Western cwm
Camp 3

Camp 2
Camp 1

Ice fall

Base Camp

Tangbotje
monastery

Kathmandu

1 Make a list of the leadership qualities that Bonington
displayed on the expedition.

2 Sum up the reasons for the expedition's success.

# 2 The company

Everest Pumps Ltd is a manufacturer of water pumping equipment with over 50 years' experience in the U.K. market. Situated in Bradford in northern England, the company was bought by a new owner after the death of the founder John Everest. The new owner was Rupert Boswell, a tough, determined accountant who decided that the company had to enter the export market to ensure its survival. In the period following his takeover Boswell replaced many of the company's original workforce with younger people, taken mainly from Bradford's Asian community. Having organized what he considered to be a new, efficient production base, Boswell began to recruit his sales, production and research team to lead the company into its newly targetted export market, the Middle East.

1 Study the organization chart below.

2 Describe the various functions for each group in the chart.

3 Predict some of the problems that might exist within and between the various groups.

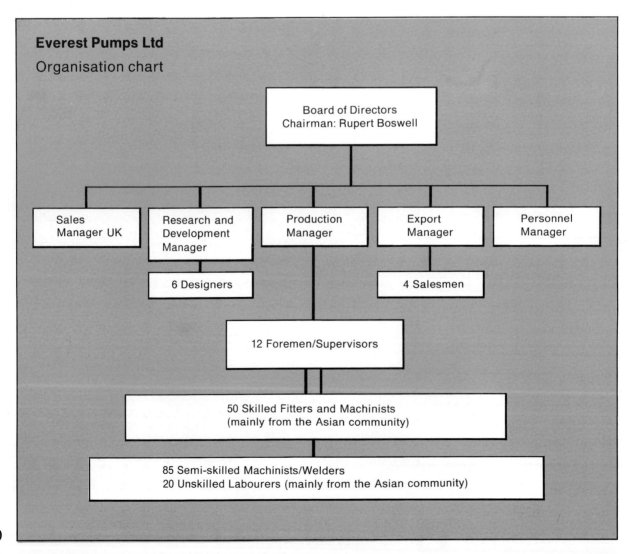

**Everest Pumps Ltd**

Organisation chart

- Board of Directors
  Chairman: Rupert Boswell
  - Sales Manager UK
  - Research and Development Manager
    - 6 Designers
  - Production Manager
    - 12 Foremen/Supervisors
      - 50 Skilled Fitters and Machinists (mainly from the Asian community)
      - 85 Semi-skilled Machinists/Welders
        20 Unskilled Labourers (mainly from the Asian community)
  - Export Manager
    - 4 Salesmen
  - Personnel Manager

# Boswell's plan

1 Study Boswell's plan for the production and sale of the new pumps.

2 Listen to his account of each stage of the plan.

3 List the problems he had to face at each stage.

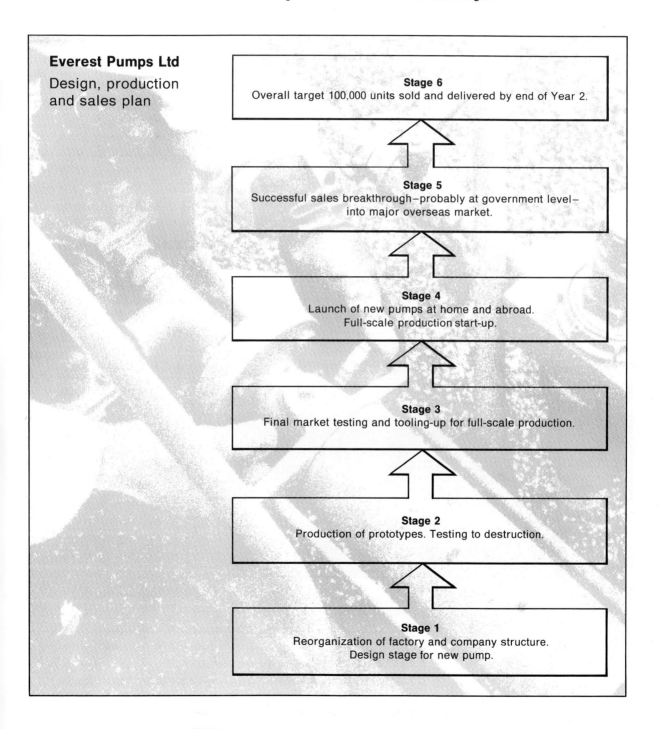

**Everest Pumps Ltd**

Design, production and sales plan

**Stage 6**
Overall target 100,000 units sold and delivered by end of Year 2.

**Stage 5**
Successful sales breakthrough—probably at government level—into major overseas market.

**Stage 4**
Launch of new pumps at home and abroad.
Full-scale production start-up.

**Stage 3**
Final market testing and tooling-up for full-scale production.

**Stage 2**
Production of prototypes. Testing to destruction.

**Stage 1**
Reorganization of factory and company structure.
Design stage for new pump.

1 Make a list of the qualities that Boswell displayed during the project.

2 Sum up the reasons for the failure of the project.

# A question of leadership

The qualities of leadership needed for effective management are the subject of a lot of debate today. One way of comparing different management approaches has been suggested by two American researchers. It is called the Managerial Grid.

1 Study the Managerial Grid below.

2 Use as many of the words below to describe the following positions on the grid.
   1.9.   5.5.   1.1.   9.1.   9.9.

3 Decide where you would place Chris Bonington and Rupert Boswell on the grid. Summarize their qualities.

4 Discuss how you would have handled Boswell's project in the light of Bonington's success and the Management Grid approach.

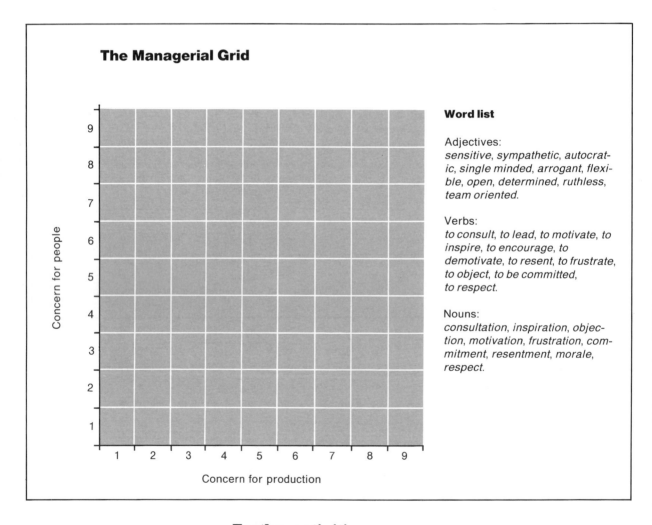

### The Managerial Grid

*(vertical axis: Concern for people, 1–9; horizontal axis: Concern for production, 1–9)*

**Word list**

Adjectives:
*sensitive, sympathetic, autocratic, single minded, arrogant, flexible, open, determined, ruthless, team oriented.*

Verbs:
*to consult, to lead, to motivate, to inspire, to encourage, to demotivate, to resent, to frustrate, to object, to be committed, to respect.*

Nouns:
*consultation, inspiration, objection, motivation, frustration, commitment, resentment, morale, respect.*

## Further activities

1 Where would you place your company's style of management on the above grid?

2 Where would you place either a) yourself or b) your boss, on the above grid?

3 Decide what the best possible position on the grid is and decide how you would change your company or department in order to achieve it?

# A short course in leadership

1 The six most important words:

   *I admit that I was wrong.*

2 The five most important words:

   *You did a great job.*

3 The four most important words:

   *What do you think?*

4 The three most important words:

   *Could you please . . .?*

5 The two most important words:

   *Thank you.*

6 The most important word:

   *We.*

7 The least important word:

   *I.*

Discuss the various human qualities suggested by each
of the sentences and words above.

Measure someone you know in your business or
private life against these various qualities.

# New formula Miracle

## UNIT 4

A new washing powder has great success until consumers begin to complain.

1 Study the new product below.

2 Present the product's features.

weight

size

3.1 kg - E10 size

brand name

**New formula**

**Miracle**

*Whiter - cleaner than ever*

**New formula**

**New low temperature washes**

**More economy**

**Cleaner**

**Whiter**

new pack design to emphasize major new selling point- economy washes

some of the major selling points of the new powder

Uniwhite trade mark

HOW TO GET THE BEST RESULTS

☐ ALL TEMPERATURES

☐ ALL MACHINES

☐ ALL FABRICS

with *Bioboost*

the new feature

Uniwhite is Britain's largest producer of household detergents. Twelve months ago the market share of its best selling *Miracle* soap powder began to fall. The message was clear. Adapt the product to the market or lose that market leader position.

**New Formula Miracle**

Uniwhite's Research and Marketing Departments responded quickly to the challenge. Within a year *New Formula Miracle* was on the market and breaking all previous records. Advance orders were higher than for any previous launch and stocks were disappearing from supermarket shelves at an unprecedented rate. For Uniwhite's Marketing Department, it was the culmination of months of careful product and market testing. For James Toft, Uniwhite's Marketing Director, and John Grant, its Senior Brand Manager, it was a personal success.

# Background: from hot washes to cold washes

Uniwhite's original *Miracle* was launched ten years ago. It steadily built up a 51% share of the household detergents market until developments in washing machine technology brought new demands from the housewife. The main development was the introduction of low temperature washing facilities. This allowed the housewife to wash clothes at 40°C which is much kinder to clothes and more economical for the housewife. Original *Miracle* however was for use in hot water and performed poorly in cold water. The loss of market share – down 17% in one year – indicated the need for urgent action.

*New Formula Miracle* contains an enzyme which allows it to remove dirt efficiently in low temperature washes. An enzyme is a biological agent which reacts with dirt particles to release them from clothing fibres. Other manufacturers had introduced enzyme powders in recent years and these powders now accounted for about 30% of the market. Uniwhite however expected this share to grow steadily as more low temperature machines were sold. Uniwhite knew that other manufacturers had had problems with their enzyme powders. Maslow and Scott, their main competitor had had to close their factory for three days and issue their workers with special gloves to prevent skin irritation. For reasons such as these, Uniwhite decided not to use the word *enzyme* on its new publicity material for *New Formula Miracle*. On the advice of their advertising agency, a low key approach to the secret behind *New Formula Miracle's* cleaning and whitening power was adopted.

1 Study Uniwhite's *New Formula Miracle* Launch Programme below.

2 Identify the missing information.

3 Listen to James Toft describe the launch programme and fill in the missing information.

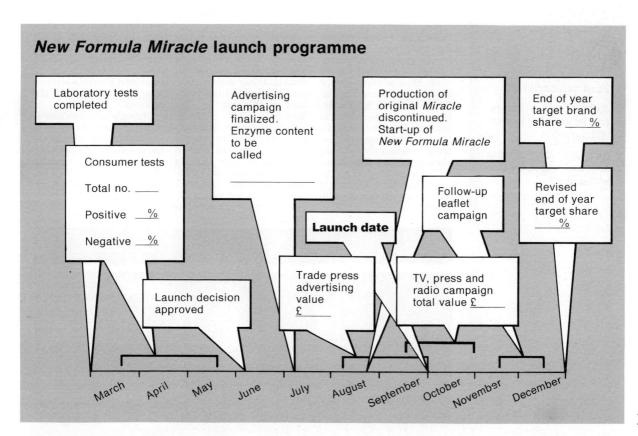

## *New Formula Miracle* launch programme

Laboratory tests completed

Consumer tests

Total no. ____

Positive ____ %

Negative ____ %

Launch decision approved

Advertising campaign finalized. Enzyme content to be called

_____

Trade press advertising value £ ____

**Launch date**

Production of original *Miracle* discontinued. Start-up of *New Formula Miracle*

Follow-up leaflet campaign

TV, press and radio campaign total value £ ____

End of year target brand share ____ %

Revised end of year target share ____ %

March April May June July August September October November December

# New Formula Miracle runs into trouble

The first sign that something was wrong came in a telephone call from a national newspaper at the end of October. To Dianne Sherrin, Uniwhite's P.R. Officer, the journalist's questions about content labelling seemed unusually well informed. Sherrin told her that the technical specification of *New Formula Miracle* was a commercial secret but that the powder had been fully tested in the market and was quite safe. Even so, Sherrin had a feeling that she had not heard the last of the matter. The next day her fears were confirmed.

1 Read the article.

2 As Dianne Sherrin, present its contents to your colleagues.

3 As a team, discuss what action to take in the face of this article.

# The big itch in your washing powder

*From our consumer affairs correspondent*

CONSUMER organizations throughout **the country are reporting a sudden increase in complaints about biological washing powders. The main target of these complaints has been New Formula Miracle, launched only a month ago with a massive television advertising campaign.**

Although not stated on the packet New Formula Miracle contains an enzyme which, consumers are saying, is causing various skin conditions, from irritation and itching to serious rashes. Housewives all over Britain have been contacting their local consumer groups and medical practitioners to see what can be done. Most of these groups have been advising those affected to switch to non-biological powders such as Max and Bril. The manufacturers insist however that their exhaustive tests showed no danger to skin.

The latest development in the affair came last night when the National Skin Council, a voluntary body which advises and supports those with sensitive skins, announced that it was withdrawing its six year old recommendation for Miracle washing powder. A spokesman confirmed that their own independent tests had shown a much higher skin response to New Formula Miracle than for the original Miracle for which their recommendation had been intended. He cited one case where a mother of three had reported rashes on two of her children after they had worn clothes recently washed in New Formula Miracle.

So far Uniwhite, the manufacturers of New Formula Miracle, have refused to comment in detail upon the reports. Other manufacturers have had similar problems in the past. In 1984 Maslow and Scott, Uniwhite's main competitor, introduced an enzyme based powder but had to withdraw it after workers complained about skin problems. The product has since been relaunched with a different enzyme and now has about 10% of the market.

The use of enzymes has been controversial ever since clothes manufacturers began to use synthetic fibres which wash best at low temperatures and require the use of biological agents to ensure the removal of all dirt. Washing machine manufacturers then introduced the special economy wash facility which allowed housewives to use water direct from the cold tap thus reducing the cost of the wash.

Until recently Uniwhite had been happy to continue with their original non-biological powder. But in the last year its market share has been shrinking rapidly due to increased competition. New Formula Miracle was their answer to the problem.

The only question now is whether there really is a problem in their new washing powder or whether a few consumers with sensitive skins and loud voices are making a fuss about relatively little.

# Crisis!

In spite of various actions taken after the first newspaper article, events began to overtake Uniwhite's *Miracle* team. On December 1st James Toft called an emergency meeting to analyze the problem. Toft presented the overall sales figures and Stephen Mills, the Advertising and Promotions Manager, presented the advertising campaign and its effects. After that, Dianne Sherrin presented the further press attention.

1 Study the diagram below.

2 As James Toft, present the recent history of *New Formula Miracle* sales on a week by week basis.

3 As Stephen Mills, present your advertising campaign week by week.

4 As Dianne Sherrin, present the press interest in *Miracle*.

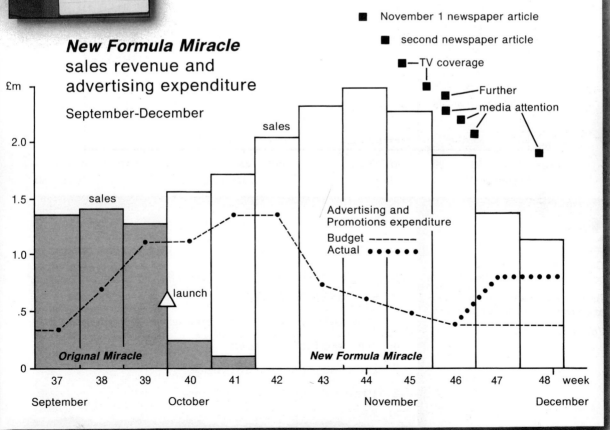

1 Listen to part of the discussion that took place during the early stages of the meeting.

2 Present Dianne Sherrin's overall argument.

Finally, James Toft asked John Grant to present the overall market situation as it had developed since early September.

1 Study the diagram below.

2 As John Grant, present the market share changes on a week by week basis.

3 Give any explanations you may have for these changes.

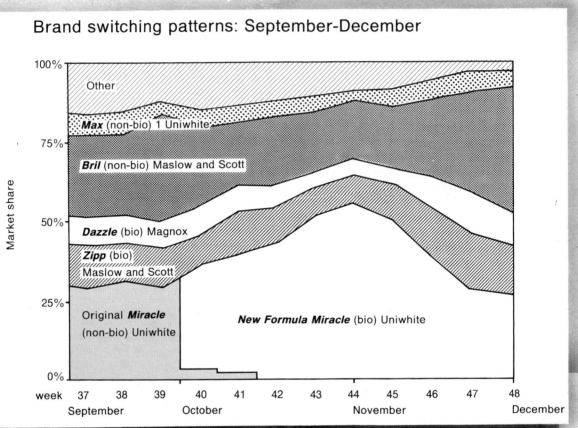

## Brand switching patterns: September–December

Market share

- Other
- **Max** (non-bio) 1 Uniwhite
- **Bril** (non-bio) Maslow and Scott
- **Dazzle** (bio) Magnox
- **Zipp** (bio) Maslow and Scott
- Original **Miracle** (non-bio) Uniwhite
- **New Formula Miracle** (bio) Uniwhite

100% — 75% — 50% — 25% — 0%

week 37 38 39 40 41 42 43 44 45 46 47 48
September          October                November              December

1 Call a meeting to analyze and solve the problems of Uniwhite.

2 Assume the different roles above and argue your various positions.

3 Follow the agenda.

A G E N D A
_____

1  The present market situation and forecasts

2  The media problem

3  The sales, marketing and advertising problem

4  The product problem

5  Options open to Uniwhite

6  Plan of action

# *New Formula Miracle*: Decision

Below are some of the options open to Uniwhite. If you wish, consider them and argue them out during your crisis meeting. Make sure that your final decisions do not conflict with each other.

| Areas of responsibility | Options | | |
|---|---|---|---|
| **1 Product** | 1<br>Leave *New Formula Miracle* unchanged | 2<br>Reduce enzyme content and announce this to press | 3<br>Quietly reduce enzyme content |
| **2 Advertising, promotion, packaging** | 1<br>Increase current advertising to counteract adverse image | 2<br>Change current ads to stress the safety of *New Formula Miracle* for normal skins | 3<br>Reduce current advertising and move to door-to-door, selling special promotions |
| **3 Press and public relations** | 1<br>Deny there is any problem with the *New Formula Miracle* | 2<br>Admit there is a problem with some skins and assure public of a solution soon | 3<br>Deny problem but offer refunds and recommend alternative non-bio powder *Max* |
| **4 Strategy** | 1<br>Continue original strategy and wait for storm to blow over | 2<br>Withdraw *New Formula Miracle* altogether and reintroduce original *Miracle* | 3<br>Reintroduce original *Miracle* and run it with *New Formula Miracle* |

**REPORT**

1 Write a press release to inform the public of your decisions.

2 Write an internal memorandum to your senior sales force telling them what they need to know about your decisions and suggesting the best way to handle things.

3 On the basis of your decisions above, write a standard letter for storage on your word processor which can be used as a reply to any further customer complaints about *New Formula Miracle*.

4 Write a formal report to your Board of Directors outlining the problem and justifying the solutions you have devised.

# Tinker, tailor, soldier, sailor . . .

To help industry and government to monitor trends in social status and class in Britain the National Readership Survey (NRS) devised a system of categorising different professions. The categories are described below. You will also find figures to show how the population has changed with regard to these categories over the last 23 years. What are the causes of these trends and how do they compare with trends in your own country?

### Grade A households – upper middle class

| | |
|---|---|
| doctors, surgeons, | university professors |
| solicitors and barristers | editors of newspapers |
| architects, surveyors, accountants | airline pilots |
| headmasters of large schools | captains of large ships |
| senior civil servants | senior executives |

| | |
|---|---|
| 1962 | **3.1%** |
| 1984 | **3%** |

### Grade B households – middle class

| | |
|---|---|
| headteachers of schools with fewer than 750 pupils | technicians with degrees |
| | air traffic controllers |
| middle rank civil servants | managers |
| university lecturers | |
| journalists | |

| | |
|---|---|
| 1962 | **13.4%** |
| 1984 | **14%** |

### Grade C1 households – lower middle class

teachers
bank clerks
civil servant (clerical grades)
student on grant

| | |
|---|---|
| 1962 | **22%** |
| 1984 | **22%** |

### Grade C2 households – skilled working class

| | |
|---|---|
| foremen | skilled engineering workers |
| charge hands | skilled mine workers |
| supervisors | |
| skilled agricultural workers | |
| bricklayers | |

| | |
|---|---|
| 1962 | **32.2%** |
| 1984 | **28%** |

### Grade D households – semi-skilled and unskilled working class

| | |
|---|---|
| most semi and unskilled labour | cleaners |
| labourers and mates of C2 grades | gardeners |
| apprentices to skilled grades | |
| most agricultural workers | |
| fishermen | |

| | |
|---|---|
| 1962 | **20.3%** |
| 1984 | **18%** |

### Grade E households – those at the lowest level of subsistence

casual labourers
old age pensioners
widows
people dependent on sickness, unemployment and supplementary benefits

| | |
|---|---|
| 1962 | **9%** |
| 1984 | **15%** |

# Fleet Street

**UNIT 5**

Analyzing Britain's national press and finding a gap in the market.

The place is Fleet Street, traditional home of Britain's national press. A revolution has just taken place in newspaper publishing. Before the revolution some publishers could not make a profit on a daily circulation of 1.5m copies. Now, with the introduction of computerized technology and advanced working practices, newspaper owners can break even with circulations of around 600,000. The implications of this are dramatic. With the right product, the chances of breaking into this once impregnable market have never looked so good. The only question for aspiring press barons is, *what* is the right product?

1 Look through and study some recent editions of Britain's daily newspapers. Identify them on the chart below which shows average daily circulation.

2 Identify the various sectors of the market.

3 Calculate the total circulation figures for each of the sectors you have identified.

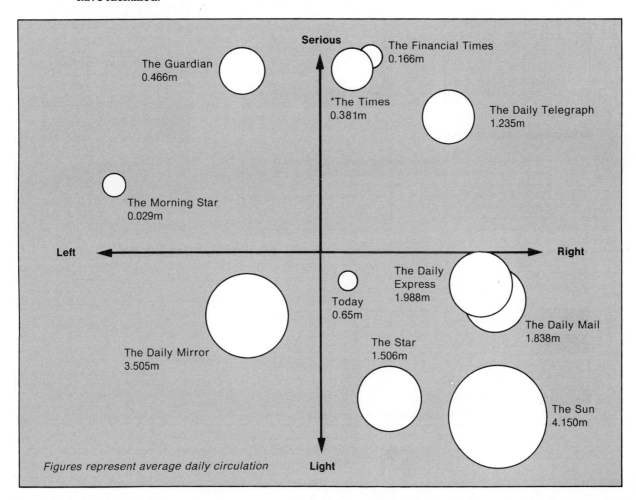

The Guardian 0.466m

**Serious**

The Financial Times 0.166m

*The Times 0.381m

The Daily Telegraph 1.235m

The Morning Star 0.029m

**Left** — **Right**

Today 0.65m

The Daily Express 1.988m

The Daily Mail 1.838m

The Daily Mirror 3.505m

The Star 1.506m

The Sun 4.150m

*Figures represent average daily circulation*

**Light**

21

Recent estimates suggest that with the latest technology which will allow journalists to type their stories directly to a computerized printing terminal, a newspaper could break even with only 600,000 copies per day. The only problem for anyone wanting to launch a new national daily is what kind of paper to produce. The obvious place to begin is by doing a little bit of market research. Imagine you are a potential newspaper owner. Look at the information below and then carry out some of your own research.

1 Study the contents of the 3 papers below.

2 Identify the contents that they have in common.

3 List their major differences.

## Britain's Dailies – the contents *

| The Sun | The Daily Express | The Guardian |
|---|---|---|

### Key

| | National News | | Business & Finance |
|---|---|---|---|
| | International News | | Sport, Entertainment, Competitions, etc. |
| | Human Interest | | Background Articles & Comment |
| | Pictures & Headlines | | Advertising |

*calculated on the basis of use of space available

1 Select one of the current newspapers you studied earlier and analyze its contents.

2 Try to describe the views and needs of its typical reader.

# Your daily paper – all is revealed!

1 Identify the newspaper you are studying in the charts below.

2 Describe the sort of people who read that paper in terms of social class.

3 Describe the sort of people who read that paper in terms of age.

## Who reads what?

Readership by social status

| Class Profile | Daily Mirror | Sun | Daily Mail | Daily Express | Daily Star | Daily Telegraph | Guardian | Times | Financial Times | Overall Population |
|---|---|---|---|---|---|---|---|---|---|---|
| A | 1 | 1 | 4 | 3 | 1 | 13 | 7 | 15 | 15 | 3 |
| B | 7 | 5 | 21 | 18 | 4 | 40 | 42 | 42 | 40 | 14 |
| C1 | 19 | 17 | 31 | 30 | 14 | 29 | 29 | 27 | 32 | 22 |
| C2 | 36 | 37 | 26 | 28 | 38 | 10 | 13 | 9 | 8 | 29 |
| D | 25 | 26 | 11 | 14 | 28 | 5 | 6 | 5 | 5 | 19 |
| E | 12 | 14 | 7 | 7 | 15 | 3 | 3 | 2 | 0 | 13 |
| Total | 100 | 100 | 100 | 100 | 100 | 100 | 100 | 100 | 100 | 100 |

Class Profile Categories:
A – upper middle class     B – middle class     C1 – lower middle class

C2 – skilled working class     D – semi-skilled and unskilled working class     E – those at the lowest level of subsistence.

Source: NRS

## Does age make a difference?

Readership by age

| Age Profile | Daily Mirror | Sun | Daily Mail | Daily Express | Daily Star | Daily Telegraph | Guardian | Times | Financial Times | Overall Population |
|---|---|---|---|---|---|---|---|---|---|---|
| 15–24 | 22 | 27 | 18 | 17 | 28 | 12 | 24 | 20 | 17 | 20 |
| 25–34 | 17 | 19 | 16 | 14 | 22 | 11 | 23 | 20 | 18 | 17 |
| 35–44 | 17 | 16 | 17 | 17 | 15 | 18 | 20 | 21 | 30 | 17 |
| 45–54 | 15 | 14 | 15 | 16 | 13 | 19 | 16 | 18 | 18 | 14 |
| 55–64 | 14 | 12 | 15 | 17 | 12 | 18 | 10 | 11 | 11 | 14 |
| 65+ | 15 | 12 | 19 | 19 | 10 | 22 | 7 | 10 | 6 | 18 |
|  | 100 | 100 | 100 | 100 | 100 | 100 | 100 | 100 | 100 | 100 |

# Watch this space!

Many of the famous newspaper owners in Fleet Street entered the business for more complex motives than profit alone. There is considerable status attached to owning a paper. There is also the possibility of influencing the nation's affairs. Some have a genuine desire to reform. Others a genuine desire to rediscover old values. From what you now know of Britain's press, decide what kind of paper you would produce if you had the opportunity.

Assume you could break even on a daily circulation of 600,000.

1 Decide what your objectives as a newspaper owner are.

2 Fill in the details below with a view to achieving those objectives.

---

**1 The target reader**

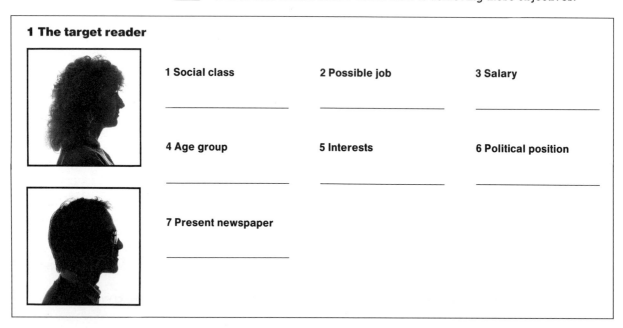

1 Social class
_____

2 Possible job
_____

3 Salary
_____

4 Age group
_____

5 Interests
_____

6 Political position
_____

7 Present newspaper
_____

---

**2 The newspaper**

Name
_____

Target circulation
per day
_____

Price
_____

Political position
_____

Special features
_____

# Some items of late news

1 Study the two diagrams below.

2 Use the information in them to make any final adjustments to your new newspaper.

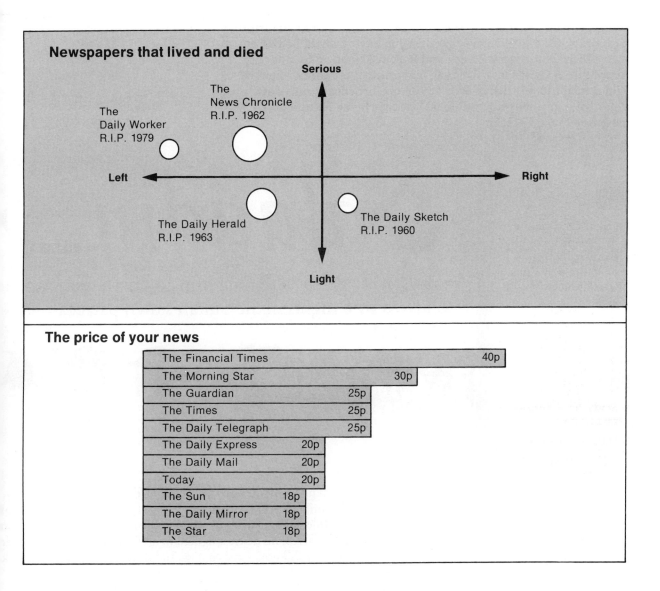

## Newspapers that lived and died

Serious

The
News Chronicle
R.I.P. 1962

The
Daily Worker
R.I.P. 1979

Left — Right

The Daily Herald
R.I.P. 1963

The Daily Sketch
R.I.P. 1960

Light

## The price of your news

| | |
|---|---|
| The Financial Times | 40p |
| The Morning Star | 30p |
| The Guardian | 25p |
| The Times | 25p |
| The Daily Telegraph | 25p |
| The Daily Express | 20p |
| The Daily Mail | 20p |
| Today | 20p |
| The Sun | 18p |
| The Daily Mirror | 18p |
| The Star | 18p |

1 Design the front page of your own newspaper.

2 Make a formal presentation of your new newspaper to your colleagues including content, target readership and political position.

**REPORT**

1 Write your first editorial page setting out your aims, hopes and editorial direction of your new newspaper.

2 Write a formal proposal to a potential financial backer of your new newspaper. Outline all the elements of the paper that you think will allow him to make a decision to back you or otherwise.

# Adventure Holidays International

A highly original holiday company upsets some very important people.

**A Recipe for Success**: The original idea was bold and simple. Make people work for their pleasure and their pleasure, when it comes, will be that much greater. Add some adventure and history, package it all as an inclusive tour and you have a world beater on your hands! For Jeremy Hunter and Rasoul Alwan, co-founders of Adventure Holidays International, that original recipe had paid off. With 4 major itineraries in their adventure brochure and a new sister company offering traditional holidays in the Middle East, the future looked bright.

1 Listen to the radio advertisement for AHI.

2 Describe the kind of people to whom such an advertisement would appeal.

1 Study the advertisement below.

2 Describe the itinerary and the events that will take place.

# Saladdin

5 days in the desert with Saladdin and his famous warrie followed by 8 nights in the Sultan's own palace.

SALADDIN (Salah ud Din), the respected enemy of the Crusaders, is remembered by history for his brilliance and daring. He was the founder of a dynasty of sul tans who for a century ruled most of the land which is present day Afaria. Now you can travel with Saladdin across his desert kingdom to his favourite palace on the edg of the Mediterranean. You will need some courage and determination. But just look the rewards.

Your adventure begins at the notorious Wadi Malaf oasis where Ibn Makluk massacred his thousand slaves. You take delivery of your very own camel and travel 5 days along the famous northern caravan route. En route you will visit the fabulous Kharoumi caves, sleep under canvas for 5 Saharan nights and find out what it's like be raided by the Wakhoubi tribe. Then you will climb the Maraba mountains befo descending to the glittering palace of the Sultan himself. Here you will enter the secr of palace life, survive a palace coup, conspire with the sultan's bodyguard . . . and finally overthrow the Sultan himself.

# AHI – the best year yet

With an advertising campaign larger than ever before now in full swing, Hunter and Alwan were expecting a bumper year. Already bookings on their established adventure itineraries and Middle East holidays were ahead of previous years and even their new route was establishing itself.

## Adventure Holidays International/Middle East Holidays

AHI

### Itinerary 2
## CAESAR
Cross the Rubicon with Caesar
10 days march on Rome + 5 nights at the baths of Caligula
£850

### Itinerary 3
## ALEXANDER
*New! New this season!*
March with Alexander from Troy to the siege of Tyre and Sidon
21 days + 7 days at the Palace of Biblos
£1050

### Itinerary 4
## ISOBEL
March on Granada with Isobel and Ferdinand
5 days + 3 days in Granada
£350

### Itinerary 1
## SALADDIN
Trek across the desert with Salah Ud Din.
5 days + 8 days in a sultan's palace. Still our most famous and popular itinerary.
£550

MEH

*Middle East Holidays*
Centres in Dubai, Qatar, Kuwait, Abu Dhabi and Oman

1 Study the range of holidays now offered by the two sister companies.

2 Relate these to the booking situation below.

3 Make a list of the unfilled capacity so far.

## Adventure Holidays International and Middle East Holidays: BOOKINGS

Places available and bookings to date on all itineraries

| Adventure Holidays | Places MAY | Bookings | Places JUNE | Bookings | Places JULY | Bookings | Places AUG–DEC | Bookings |
|---|---|---|---|---|---|---|---|---|
| 1 Saladdin | 120 | 115 | 250 | 230 | 300 | 310 | 500 | 250 |
| 2 Caesar | 50 | 30 | 90 | 75 | 120 | 90 | 150 | 90 |
| 3 Alexander | 50 | 10 | 120 | 30 | 120 | 45 | 200 | 30 |
| 4 Isobel | 90 | 50 | 90 | 75 | 90 | 80 | 200 | 120 |
| Middle East Holidays | 400 | 315 | 500 | 350 | 600 | 450 | 1000 | 250 |

# Crisis!

On the day that Alwan was due to fly out to visit some of their Middle East holiday locations, the following newspaper article appeared.

1 Read the newspaper article below.

2 Identify the problem that now faces AHI.

3 Suggest a list of immediate actions that AHI should take.

APRIL 29th

# Afaria clamps down on cultural exploitation

FROM OUR TRAVEL CORRESPONDENT

The government of Afaria has introduced tough new laws to stop what it calls cultural distortion and exploitation. Announcing the new measures in parliament today, the Minister of Culture, Ali M. Raouf, referred to a number of examples where his country's long traditions and beliefs were being exploited by profit-hungry foreign nationals and companies.

One of the main targets of the new rules is the tourist industry which encourages foreigners to come to Afaria to enjoy what Mr Raouf called a totally incorrect view of his country's past. He gave one example of tribespeople being asked to perform different kinds of activities to entertain foreign tourists. In one case tribesmen had to '*raid*' the tourist party as if they were bandits and then allow themselves to be attacked when the tourists had their '*revenge*'. Mr Raouf said such activities were degrading and humiliating and were a form of cultural pornography. These activities had to cease immediately. Companies guilty of such activities would be banned.

It is widely believed here that the main offender is Adventure Holidays International, a London based operation that arranges 'unexpected events during its adventure holidays in Afaria. Its Saladdin tour contains a Bedouin 'raid' and a 'Palace Coup' to entertain and excite its clients. Local people are employed to perform such parts as palace guards, harem attendants and brutal sultans.

Mr Raouf also claims that much of such companies' publicity contains historical and cultural inaccuracies. Salah ud Din, for example, never visited this part of the world and certainly never had a palace there.

The government of Afaria is considering approaching neighbouring governments with a view to boycotting the offending companies.

Last night it was reported that the local representative of Adventure Holidays International in Afaria had been detained under the new laws. So far Adventure Holidays International Headquarters in London have made no comment on the affair.

# The last letter from Afaria

At the meeting called to act on the crisis, Rasoul Alwan produced a letter he had received only two days before from Paul Harding, AHI's representative in Afaria.

1 Read the letter.

2 Describe Harding's interpretation of the situation.

3 From all the available evidence so far, decide what the most likely situation is now in Afaria.

The Maguire Hotel
Afaria Town

20 April

Dear Rasoul,

I just thought I'd drop you a line to let you know what's happening out here. We had the first three groups through two weeks ago and everything went very well. We have two more groups in the desert at the moment.

My main worry is about the present political situation here. Since the assassination, the government has been playing a very clever game. They're clearly afraid of the surge of tribal and religious sentiment and are having to make concessions. One of these has been to give one of the country's main religious leaders a seat in the cabinet. So far there have been no obvious changes in the way things run. The country still has serious economic difficulties and it's my feeling that these worries will eventually limit the powers of the religious and ethnic parties. So don't take what you hear at face value. There's a lot of posturing going on and it will take time to sort itself out.

By the way, I recently heard that we have some competition just across the border in Moccala. A company calling itself  is running similar tours to ours. Their address is somewhere in Kent. Perhaps we should send in the Wakhoubi! That's all for now. See you at the end of the season.

Best wishes,

Paul

## AGENDA

1  Clarification of the situation in Afaria

2  Possible concessions

3  Impact of ban on AHI

4  Impact of boycott

5  Long-term policy in the region

6  Action

Call a meeting of AHI to discuss the crisis and decide on a plan of action. Use this agenda.

# Yamacom

## A marriage is announced

The merger between two major names in the world of computers and telecommunications caused a sensation when it was announced. On paper the potential power of the new alliance was immense. In the real world, however, the fact that one of the companies, Transcom Inc, was American and the other, Yamahata K K, was Japanese, caused raised eyebrows on both sides of the Pacific.

UNIT 7

A Japanese and an American company fail to reap benefits from trans-Pacific co-operation.

1  Study the advertisement below.

2  Identify the advantages of the merger for Transcom Inc.

3  Identify the advantages of the merger for Yamahata K K.

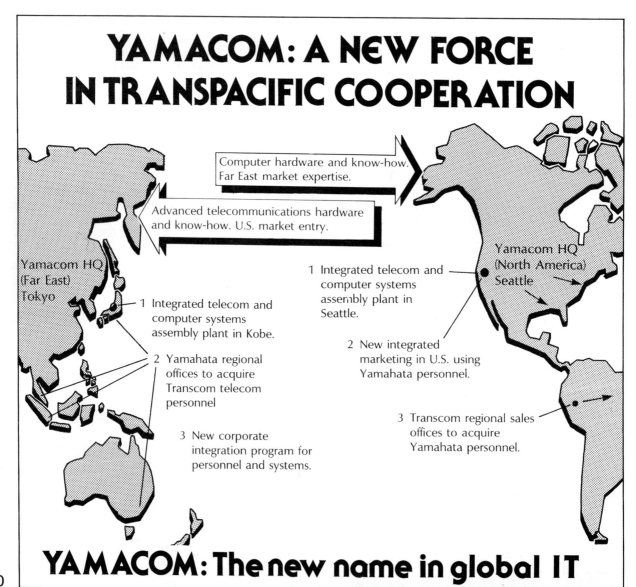

30

# A people problem

The outside world heard little of what was happening in the new company during the first year of the merger. There were some wry smiles from Yamacom's competitors when rumours began to surface about trouble in the new company's Far East markets. The main problem seemed to centre on Indonesia. Stories began to emerge from the Jakarta office of breakdowns in communication, cross-cultural rivalry and sometimes actual blocking of progress of one department by another. Sales figures for the office were actually down on pre-merger days. It was while Mark Weinberg, Yamacom's Regional Director, was in Jakarta investigating the sales problem that he overheard the following conversation between Paul Mackowitz and Hiroshi Watanabe, two Yamacom employees.

1  Listen to the conversation between Mackowitz and Watanabe.

2  Identify the reasons why Mackowitz sacked Shigeta.

3  Identify some of the cultural problems that separated the American from his Japanese colleagues.

On his return to the Central Office, Weinberg reported his feelings and impressions to the Liaison Committee monitoring the merger. Six weeks later Area Managers were called to a special seminar in Nagoya. At this seminar a world authority on Japanese-American cultural differences presented a paper which was summed up in the following hand-out.

1  Study the comparison below.

2  Use some of the words in the comparison to explain Mackowitz's behaviour in the conversation you have just heard.

3  Use some of the words in the comparison to explain Shigeta's and Watanabe's behaviour.

---

**Contrasts in Culture, Tradition and Behaviour between Japanese and US citizens**

| United States | Japan |
|---|---|
| 1 Individualistic culture | 1 Collective culture |
| 2 Independent attitudes | 2 Dependent attitudes |
| 3 Authoritative decision making | 3 Participative decision making |
| 4 Competitive ethic | 4 Cooperative ethic |
| 5 Style: Confrontation | 5 Style: Compromise |
| 6 Decision making quick but implementation slow | 6 Decision making slow but implementation quick |
| 7 Personal relationships – direct | 7 Personal relationships – indirect |
| 8 World view – short term | 8 World view – long term |
| 9 Communications are one-way and secretive | 9 Communications are interactive and open |
| 10 Companies emphasise efficiency | 10 Companies emphasise effectiveness |
| 11 Main management function is control | 11 Main management function is to serve the customer |
| 12 High job mobility | 12 Life long employment |
| 13 Low company loyalty | 13 High company loyalty |
| 14 Incompetence is fatal | 14 Shame is fatal |
| 15 Society is heterogeneous | 15 Society is homogeneous |
| 16 Attitudes are relaxed and casual | 16 Attitudes are tense and formal |
| 17 The specialist is valued highly | 17 The generalist is valued highly |
| 18 Freedom and equality are valued highly | 18 Order and hierarchy are valued highly |

Adapted from Chikara Higashi – World Bank

---

1  Listen to the expert answering questions from the participants at the seminar about cross-cultural problems.

2  List some of the tips the speaker gives to American businessmen going to Japan for the first time.

3  Make a list of similar tips for a Japanese businessman visiting America or Europe for the first time.

# A new beginning in Jakarta

After a very pleasant week at the Nagoya seminar, Weinberg had to face the real world again when he returned to the Central Office. The Jakarta situation had reached a new crisis. No one, it seemed, was talking to Mackowitz any more and the morale in the territory was at an all time low. Weinberg made the decision to re-call Mackowitz there and then. Two days later an internal memo was circulated around the Yamacom system worldwide.

# YAMACOM INTERNATIONAL

Applications are invited for the following position, to be filled internally:

GENERAL MANAGER (YAMACOM INDONESIA)

This position is to be filled by an American employee of Yamacom under the merger agreement of 1992.

Duties:

1   To report to South East Asia Divisional Director, Mr. Lee Than Quo, in Singapore.

2   To be responsible for the overall control and administration of the Indonesian subsidiary.

3   To be responsible for the financial performance of this subsidiary under guidelines set by the Divisional Director.

4   To initiate new sales systems with a view to expanding new American and Japanese multinational business in Indonesia.

5   To ensure continuing integration of staff and functions in a subsidiary at present consisting of 19 Japanese sales staff, 5 U.S. sales personnel, and 25 other technical and adminis-trative personnel of U.S., Japanese and Indonesian nationalities.

A fortnight after this a short list of candidates for Mackowitz's position had been drawn up. As Weinberg began his final assessment of the candidates, he reflected that at least the seminar and his experiences in Jakarta had given him a slightly clearer idea of what he was looking for in the personnel files now before him.

Name: Thomas Jackson

Age: 34 years

Status: Single

Present position: Senior Marketing Executive, East Coast, corporate clients

Domicile: Boston

Number of years with Transcom/Yamacom: 5

Education: Yale & Harvard

Languages: Some Spanish

Background: Graduated from Yale in Economics and from Harvard with an MBA. Spent 2 years as a fast-moving consumer goods salesman in Boston to 'get the feel of front-line action'. Joined Transcom in 1983 and piloted through integrated telecommunication packages for Realtors. Saw this side of business expand to $50 m in 2 years. Transferred to Corporate networking systems in 1985 and became Senior Marketing Exec. last year. Has seen business expand by 15% since then.

Comments: Very logical and clear-thinking and plenty of energy. Very confident and demands maximum commitment from his staff. No overseas work experience. Originally from South Carolina and a lay Southern Baptist Minister. Also trains and coaches Boston Cubs Football team.

Jackson has expressed a lot of interest in the new position but wants to know exactly what his reporting lines will be between the Jakarta office and Yamacom Central Office. He's looking for maximum freedom to develop the Indonesian territory along the same lines he built up the East Coast corporate business here. Says that an overseas position of responsibility is probably now a pre-requisite for advancement in the company now that it has 'gone international in such a big way.'

---

Name: Stephanie Martinez

Age: 36 years

Status: Divorced, 1 child

Present position: Customer Services Manager (Far East)

Domicile: Taipeh

Number of years with Transcom/Yamacom: 2

Education: Berkeley Cal.

Languages: Some Japanese

Background: After graduating from Berkeley in Comparative Literature, did a further 3 years on MBA course. Lectured in Business Studies for 2 years. She married a Japanese student and, after that, moved to Japan where she worked for Transglobe Airlines as marketing adviser for the Far East. Separated from her husband after 1 year. Left Transglobe after 2 years and joined Transcom to help set up Taipeh office. Currently in Taipeh.

Comments: A very clever woman with interests in Eastern religions. No direct sales experience. Very extrovert and intelligent. Likes change and applies for different jobs in Transcom every year.

She has been slightly eclipsed in her present position by the merger putting most of the customer services department into the hands of the old Yamahata Office in Tokyo. This is not her fault and she has done her best to get the two integrated (but has met with resistance from Tokyo since her role was not included in the original merger agreement). This was a structural oversight during the merger and the Taipeh position will be terminated next month.

Name:    Lee Miller

Age:     44 years
Status:  Divorced, no children

Present position:    Software Support
Manager, Europe

Domicile:  Frankfurt, Germany

Number of years with
Transcom/Yamacom: 14

Education:  Delaware High
School

Languages: French, German,
Chinese

Background:   He is a naturalised Taiwanese married to an American but
recently divorced. Served in the U.S. forces in Japan (1963-68) and
Vietnam (1969-74). Joined Transcom in 1975 but had one year's leave
after car accident. Trained as computer programmer with us and special-
ises in Business expert systems. Has experience in both software sales
and support. Excellent record in Europe.

Comments:   Very softly-spoken man who gets on well with Europeans. Has
adapted well to overseas assignments. Presently living with German
girlfriend.

Miller is being recommended for this position by his General Manager,
Europe. The G.M. says his oriental background will give him a lot of
credibility in the Far East.

Name:    Dan Masters Jr.

Age:     41 years
Status:  Married, 4 children

Present position:  Regional Sales
Manager for Latin America

Domicile:  Bogotá, Colombia

Number of years with
Transcom/Yamacom:  10

Education:  UCLA

Languages Spanish, Quechua (ancient
Peruvian language), Russian,
French

Background:    Graduated from UCLA in Modern Languages and was drafted into
army as intelligence officer. Spent some years in Vietnam but then became
conscientious objector and spent several years outside U.S. until the
amnesty. Lived in Peru and met his wife there. Joined Transcom in 1979
and headed Sales Office in Peru for 3 years. Became Regional Sales Manager
in 1982.

Comments:    A good leader with an excellent sales record. He is an amateur
artist and plays chess at an international level. Holds a private pilot's
license. Knows Japan well from his Vietnam days.

Masters is a very quiet man and not given to displays of emotion. Has been
criticised by some staff for not giving credit where it's due. Yet praised
by others for his loyalty and judgement in very difficult situations.
Because he's his own man, many people react badly when they first know
him. Eventually however, they accept that his judgement is excellent. Has
occasionally upset superiors by applying same standards of conduct to them
as he does to his staff. Has survived so far though!

# Final selection board

1 Study the grid below.

2 As a group, discuss the strengths and weaknesses of each candidate.

3 When you have completed your discussion, each member of the group should independently score the candidates against the criteria below. (10 = excellent   0 = very poor).

4 Announce your scores to the group and then as a group negotiate to select a final candidate from the short list.

**Interview Assessment Summary: Jakarta.**
**(Score each box 1–10)**

|  | Jackson | Martinez | Miller | Masters |
|---|---|---|---|---|
| 1 Relevant experience |  |  |  |  |
| 2 Energy and enthusiasm |  |  |  |  |
| 3 Intelligence |  |  |  |  |
| 4 Track record |  |  |  |  |
| 5 Cultural sensitivity |  |  |  |  |
| 6 Adaptability |  |  |  |  |
| 7 Cross-cultural leadership qualities |  |  |  |  |
| 8 Learning aptitude |  |  |  |  |
| 9 Judgement |  |  |  |  |
| 10 Organizational abilities |  |  |  |  |
| **Totals** |  |  |  |  |

## REPORT

1 Write a short formal report about the problems of different nationalities working with each other in the same company. Include recommendations for overcoming the problems which may arise.

2 Write a letter of introduction to the staff in Jakarta telling them about yourself and your hopes for the future of the subsidiary under your leadership.

# One man's view of European law

The following is an extract of a speech made by Newton Minnow, former Chairman of the US Federal Communications Commission, in a speech to the Association of American Law Schools.

**After 35 years I have finished a comprehensive study of European Comparative law.**

**In Germany, under the law, everything is prohibited except that which is permitted.**

**In France, under the law, everything is permitted, except that which is prohibited.**

**In the Soviet Union, under the law, everything is prohibited, including that which is permitted**

**And in Italy, under the law, everything is permitted, especially that which is prohibited.**

1 Discuss Mr Minnow's views on the laws of the countries above.

2 Discuss reasons why we develop national stereotypes and how much truth, if any, they usually contain.

# Oxfam

Oxfam is one of Britain's major relief and development agencies. Its main role is to support long-term aid projects in the Third World. Now and again these long-term projects are interrupted by major disasters. At times such as these Oxfam has to divert scarce resources and find the extra funds necessary to help the victims of floods, earthquakes and, most recently, famine.

## The news that shocked the world

The news from Ethiopia broke late in the evening of October 25.

1 Listen to the radio broadcast.
2 Describe the situation in Ethiopia.
3 Identify the people most at risk.

1 Look at the map and identify the various methods of reaching the feeding centres from Britain.
2 List the needs of the three categories of famine victims.

## UNIT 8

A major world relief agency struggles to allocate resources to famine victims.

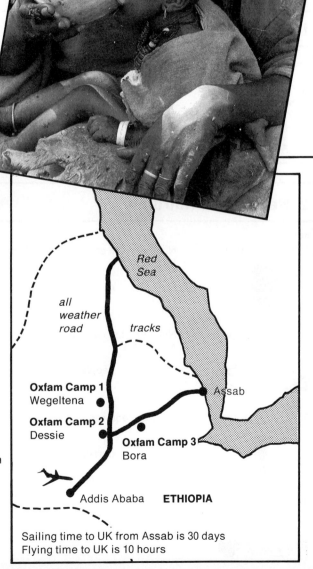

## The famine in Ethiopia

### The needs

Oxfam has three feeding centres in Ethiopia. New arrivals at these centres are weighed and measured to assess the crucial weight to height ratio. This indicates the likely needs of each individual.

1 Seriously malnourished arrivals. Less than 70% of normal weight to height ratio. Need immediate and constant care. Priorities are rehydration and non-solid, high energy feeding up to 28 days.

2 Moderately malnourished arrivals. 70–90% of normal weight to height ratio. Need feeding programme to supplement home diets. Main needs are milk, biscuit, grain and shelter.

3 Slightly malnourished arrivals. 90% of normal weight to height ratio. Need grain to bring diet up to the standard family ration of 15 kilograms per person per month.

Red Sea

all weather road

tracks

**Oxfam Camp 1**
Wegeltena

Assab

**Oxfam Camp 2**
Dessie

**Oxfam Camp 3**
Bora

Addis Ababa    **ETHIOPIA**

Sailing time to UK from Assab is 30 days
Flying time to UK is 10 hours

37

# The Emergency Unit meets

It is 8.30 the next morning. Already the news of the famine is having an impact. Money in the form of cash, cheques and credit card pledges is pouring into Oxfam's Emergency Fund. Not far away from the Fund Raising Office, Oxfam's Emergency Unit is preparing to meet to draw up a plan of action. The Unit consists of specialists from many fields. Their brief? To assess the needs of the famine victims and to allocate the limited funds to those unlimited needs.

## Background information

The average altitude of this area of Ethiopia is 1,800 metres above sea level. At night the temperature drops to below 5° Centigrade and occasionally to below freezing. During the day the temperature often rises to above 35° Centigrade. The region has very poor roads. Although there are many rivers, the rain, if and when it comes, runs away very quickly leaving the land parched and barren. There has been no real rainfall for three years. Crops have failed. The villagers have long ago eaten the seed corn for any future harvests. The only hope now is the long trek to the towns and main roads where the outside world begins.

 1 From the grid below, identify the information that the Emergency Unit will need to make its immediate decisions.

 2 Listen to the experts talking and fill in the missing information on the first three grids.

---

## 1 Food

| Item | | | Notes |
|---|---|---|---|
| 1 Grain | Number 1 ton can feed for 60 days <br><br> ..................people | Cost per metric ton <br><br> £.................... | |

---

## 2 Health and nutrition

| Item | | | Notes |
|---|---|---|---|
| 1 Powdered milk | Number 1 ton can feed for 60 days <br><br> ..................people | Cost per metric ton <br><br> £.................... | |
| 2 Oxfam energy biscuit | Number 1 ton can feed for 60 days <br><br> ..................people | Cost per metric ton <br><br> £.................... | |
| 3 Nurse/nutritionist | Number required <br><br> ..................nurses | Cost per nurse/nutritionist <br><br> £.................... | |
| 4 Equipment: Land Rovers | Number required <br><br> ..................vehicles | Cost per vehicle <br><br> £.................... | |

## 3 Shelter

| Type | Description | Cost per unit |
|------|-------------|---------------|
| 1 Blanket | 2m × 1·5m. Made of wool and synthetic fibre. Can maintain body heat down to 1°C. Weight 0·5kg. | _____ per blanket |
| 2 Plastic sheeting | 28m × 40m. Can be cut up and placed over sticks to provide cover for several family units. Weight per roll 20kgs. | _____ per roll |
| 3 Knitted clothing | Clothes knitted free of charge to Oxfam patterns. 20 items 2kgs. | Nil |

## 4 Water

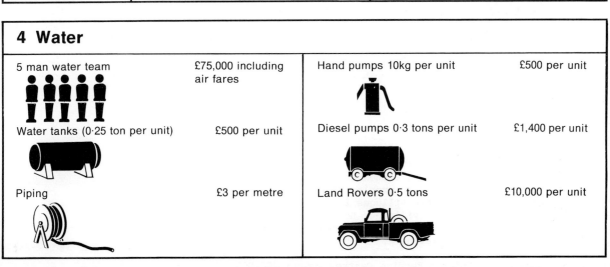

5 man water team — £75,000 including air fares

Water tanks (0·25 ton per unit) — £500 per unit

Piping — £3 per metre

Hand pumps 10kg per unit — £500 per unit

Diesel pumps 0·3 tons per unit — £1,400 per unit

Land Rovers 0·5 tons — £10,000 per unit

## 5 Personnel

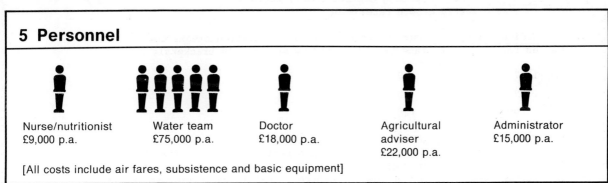

Nurse/nutritionist £9,000 p.a.

Water team £75,000 p.a.

Doctor £18,000 p.a.

Agricultural adviser £22,000 p.a.

Administrator £15,000 p.a.

[All costs include air fares, subsistence and basic equipment]

## 6 Transport

| Transport costs per metric ton | Delivery time |
|-------------------------------|---------------|
| Air £780 UK to Addis-Ababa | 10 hours |
| Land £120 Addis or Assab to feeding centres | 2 days |
| Sea £22 UK to Assab port | 30 days |

# The latest news from Britain and Ethiopia

It is now 11 am. The latest update from the Disasters Fund Office indicates an inflow of about £50,000 per hour. At this rate the Fund Manager calculates that the Emergency Unit can expect a total fund after three weeks of about £4m. At 11.10 the following telex arrives from Ethiopia.

1 Study the report and, using the previous grids, list the items needed to meet a) immediate needs, b) short to medium-term needs and c) long-term needs.

2 Calculate the amounts and values of each item that will be needed for the immediate, short to medium and long-term needs.

| Disasters Unit | Oxfam Feeding Centre |
|---|---|
| Oxfam House | Bora |
| 274 Banbury Road | Ethiopia |
| Oxford | |
| U.K. | |

FIELD REPORT OCTOBER 19

General: Situation grim. People massing at many points on main roads in search of food. Worst scenes at feeding centres due to lack of resources and overcrowding. Main problem is that success of centres is causing more people to leave villages for food. Short-term solution is to open new centres nearer villages. Long-term solution is to build up agricultural infrastructure on village-by-village basis. Water teams and seed corn essential here.

Specific: Today's Feeding Centres count: 200,000
         Weekly growth rate: +10%

Medical situation: Current Feeding Centre population breaks down as follows (percentage breakdown of new arrivals in brackets):

1   70% w/h ratio      20,000   (15%)

2   70-90% w/h ratio   40,000   (30%)

3   90% w/h ratio      140,000  (55%)

Summary: Priority needs are the immediate high-risk categories. But in long term, whole population (1m in this region alone) at risk. Essential to tackle problem at root. There are 200 villages and 10 major towns within 50-mile radius of feeding centres. That is where problem begins and where our major long-term effort should be. Detailed report to follow.

P.S. - SS Elpis arrived ahead of schedule yesterday and grain now moving inland. Thanks to all concerned.

Mark Tremaign
Bora Feeding Centre

# The Emergency Unit goes into action

The Emergency Unit reconvened at 2.30 in the afternoon. They now had the best information upon which to make their decisions.

1 Divide into three groups and allocate the following areas of responsibility: emergency needs; short to medium-term needs; long-term needs.

2 Examine the three risk categories and decide what your priorities should be for each.

3 On the chart below devise the best plan for saving the greatest number of lives within the £4m budget.

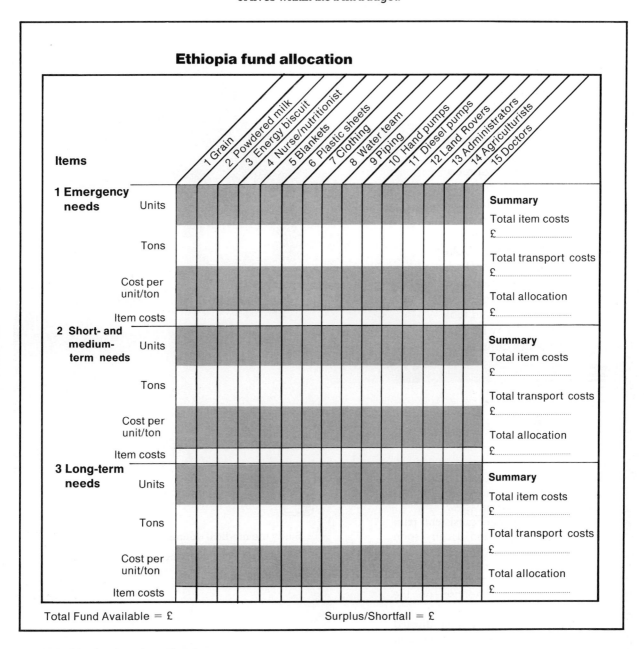

## Ethiopia fund allocation

Column headers: 1 Grain, 2 Powdered milk, 3 Energy biscuit, 4 Nurse/nutritionist, 5 Blankets, 6 Plastic sheets, 7 Clothing, 8 Water team, 9 Piping, 10 Hand pumps, 11 Diesel pumps, 12 Land Rovers, 13 Administrators, 14 Agriculturists, 15 Doctors

**Items**

**1 Emergency needs**
- Units
- Tons
- Cost per unit/ton
- Item costs

Summary
- Total item costs £
- Total transport costs £
- Total allocation £

**2 Short- and medium-term needs**
- Units
- Tons
- Cost per unit/ton
- Item costs

Summary
- Total item costs £
- Total transport costs £
- Total allocation £

**3 Long-term needs**
- Units
- Tons
- Cost per unit/ton
- Item costs

Summary
- Total item costs £
- Total transport costs £
- Total allocation £

Total Fund Available = £          Surplus/Shortfall = £

## REPORT

1 Hold a press conference to announce the actions you are taking in Ethiopia.

2 Plan and design an advertising campaign to bring more money into the Ethiopia Fund.

# A severe case of TSV

A car components manufacturer is blamed for damaging the health of its employees.

'Of what?', asked George Harmer, Managing Director of Harmer Hydraulics. 'Tenosinovitis,' said Pamela Bridges with a chuckle. 'It's a bit like tennis elbow . . .' Harmer looked across at his Personnel Officer in disbelief. 'Are you telling me that we have lost two complete shifts this week because our people are playing too much tennis?' Bridges looked slightly uncomfortable. 'No. It's nothing to do with tennis. Or their elbows for that matter. It's their hands . . . they say they have developed tenosinovitis because of the way we make them assemble our brake cylinders. And unfortunately the company doctor seems to agree.' Harmer looked suddenly tired. 'I'm sorry Pamela, I'm not quite sure I understand . . .'. Pamela Bridges opened her briefcase and took out a dictionary. 'Okay Mr Harmer, let's start with a definition . . .'

### tenosinovitis

**tenosinovitis**
An inflammation of the muscle tissue usually following repeated use or movement of the affected muscles.
*Symptoms*: Sharp and persistent pain from the affected region usually soon after use of the muscles.
*Causes*: Uncertain. Possibly due to a build up of oxidising agents in the tissues following excessive exercise of the muscles.
*Treatment*: Complete rest of the affected areas for at least 12 hours. Longer term sufferers often require longer periods of rest.

1 Study the medical definition.

2 What are the causes of the condition?

3 What is the cure?

# Background

Harmer Hydraulics produces hydraulic systems for the motor vehicle industry. A major component of these systems is a small piston consisting of a metal cylinder with two rubber seals on either end. The pistons were originally assembled at Harmer's factory using a specially designed tool which squeezes the rubber parts onto the ends of the cylinders. Using the tool, however, was a slow process and because the assembly workers were on a piece-rate system, they preferred to assemble the pistons manually. Management did not object because output was considerably higher using this method. The trouble started when a supplier began to use a stiffer rubber for the seals. Harmer's workers began to complain of sore fingers. When it was pointed out to them that they should be using the tools provided the complaints stopped. As a precaution the supplier reintroduced the original rubber part.

Shortly after this, the company announced losses for the second year running due to recession in the car industry. It meant that an attempt by the union convenor Max Smith to win a 10% wage increase for his members came to nothing. Smith was a very conscientious and hard working convenor but after this setback he became quiet and sullen. His regular Friday meetings with management became short and tense affairs and very little came out of them. For a while production continued normally. It was exactly a month after the company's announcement of the losses that a morning shift had to be cancelled because of sickness. A check of the files showed a 300% increase in sick notes in the last three weeks. And almost all the notes now contained the word *Tenosinovitis*. Bridges knew where the problem lay. Bumping into Max Smith in the corridor the next morning, she invited him for a chat in the executive suite later that day.

1 Listen to the conversation between Max Smith and Pamela Bridges.
2 Describe Max Smith's attitude.
3 Explain Pamela Bridges' arguments.

1 Read the letter below.
2 Describe the shop floor situation from the industrial relations point of view.
3 Describe the shop floor situation from the medical point of view.

## Harmer Hydraulics Ltd

```
INTERNAL MEMORANDUM

To:   George Harmer

From: Pamela Bridges
```

After seeing Max Smith today, I decided to talk to some of the people on the shop floor. My impression is that he's certainly got things stirred up there — especially among the younger workers and the women. I asked Jack Hubbard to monitor work in the assembly department for any obvious signs of pain or discomfort and he said that the pains only seemed to start when the workers were in the locker rooms.

Jack did take me to see one man whose hands were slightly swollen and who obviously suffered some pain. Two or three others also claimed to have aches and pains and seemed quite genuine. Most people, though, did not seem to want to talk about it. I did get one bloke to admit that Smith had told everyone to report any slight ache to the nurse. Apparently, he said that such aches could be the first warning signs of something more serious.

I also spoke to the company doctor. He says that with one or two obvious cases of tenosinovitis, he has no option but to give everyone who complains the benefit of the doubt. Apparently, it's very hard to diagnose the complaint without very lengthy and thorough tests.

My feeling is that we should meet the union as soon as possible and put our side of the case.

*Pam*

# A letter from the union

1 Read the letter for its gist.
2 Describe the union's present position with regard to legal action.
3 List the main union demands.

# The United Motor Workers' Union

Mr George Harmer
Managing Director
Harmer Hydraulics Ltd
Mansfield

March 12

Dear Mr Harmer,

I am writing to inform you of our intentions with respect to the complaints we have received of late from our members in your pistons section. These complaints relate to the increase in the incidence of tenosinovitis, a condition which is causing a lot of suffering and anxiety amongst our members in your factory. In the past month, we have received 30 official notifications of this condition from our members. Each notification has been accompanied by a medical certificate.

It is our view that there is irrefutable evidence that the condition is brought about by your present working practices and that these practices contravene Part I, Sections 2(1) and 2(2) and Section 6(1) of the Health and Safety at Work Act 1974. We are confident that the court would find in our favour should we decide to proceed with the matter.

We would prefer to settle this matter out of court and would suggest the following outline of an agreement:

1  That the present tools and practices are modified to avoid injury to health.

2  That the present piece-rate system is replaced by a consolidated wage rate based on the last quarter's average earnings under the present system.

3  That all our members who have suffered injury under the present working practices should receive lump sum compensation of £3000 each.

We look forward to hearing your response to our proposals.

Yours sincerely,

JDMathews

Mr J.D. Mathews
National Officer

# A question of law

Five years before, a worker at Harmer Hydraulics had slipped on a chip in the work's canteen and had won £1,500 compensation from the company. George Harmer was determined that such petty claims would never again be successful. Soon after he received the letter from the union he called in his lawyers to advise. They brought with them a copy of the relevant act.

1 Study the sections of the Health and Safety at Work Act below.

2 Explain each section of the Act in your own words.

3 Identify the sections that will help the union to win its case.

4 Identify the sections that will help the company to win its case.

---

*General duties*

General duties of employers to their employees.

**2.**—(1) It shall be the duty of every employer to ensure, so far as is reasonably practicable, the health, safety and welfare at work of all his employees.

(2) Without prejudice to the generality of an employer's duty under the preceding subsection, the matters to which that duty extends include in particular—

(a) the provision and maintenance of plant and systems of work that are, so far as is reasonably practicable, safe and without risks to health ;

(b) arrangements for ensuring, so far as is reasonably practicable, safety and absence of risks to health in connection with the use, handling, storage and transport of articles and substances ;

(c) the provision of such instruction, training and supervision as is necessary to ensure, so far as is reasonably practicable, the health and safety at work of his employees ;

---

General duties of manufacturers etc. as regards articles and substances for use at work.

**6.**—(1) It shall be the duty of any person who designs, manufactures, imports or supplies any article for use at work—

(a) to ensure, so far as is reasonably practicable, that the article is so designed and constructed as to be safe and without risks to health when properly used ;

(b) to carry out or arrange for the carrying out of such

---

General duties of employees at work.

**7.** It shall be the duty of every employee while at work—

(a) to take reasonable care for the health and safety of himself and of other persons who may be affected by his acts or omissions at work ; and

(b) as regards any duty or requirement imposed on his employer or any other person by or under any of the relevant statutory provisions, to co-operate with him so far as is necessary to enable that duty or requirement to be performed or complied with.

# Decision

1 Hold a meeting to discuss the problem facing Harmer Hydraulics.

2 Decide how the company will argue its case in court.

3 Decide how the United Motor Workers' Union will argue its case.

---

AGENDA for meeting to be held to discuss TSV problem

---

1 Review of the history of the problem.

2 Identification of the nature of the problem.

3 The costs and consequences of settling the matter out of court.

4 The benefits and the penalties of fighting the case in the courts.

5 Arguments to be used to fight the case in court.

6 Action to be taken to prevent such disputes arising in the future.

---

Divide into three groups: a) The Counsel for Harmer Hydraulics, b) The Counsel for the United Motor Workers' Union and c) The Presiding Judge.

The Presiding Judge should then open proceedings by asking the Counsel for the Union to put its case. The Counsel for Harmer Hydraulics should then present its own case. Arguments should then be submitted by both parties. Finally, the judge should sum up and pronounce a verdict.

## REPORT

1 As Managing Director of Harmer Hydraulics, write a standard letter to your employees outlining the outcome of the case and its implications for the future.

2 Write a letter from the United Motor Workers' Union announcing the outcome of the court case and discussing its implications for the future.

3 As Presiding Judge for the case, write an official report on the background to the case, your findings and any implications for the future.

# The oil rig

### A short history of Vitrasia

Vitrasia is a small country in the Gulf of Nowhere which, until recently, enjoyed one of the world's highest per capita incomes. Its wealth was based on the export of milk bottles and table knives, commodities for which the tiny country was famous the world over. After years of success, the fatal blow fell without warning. Cheap, plastic cartons and table knives from the Far East of Nowhere began to flood Vitrasia's traditional markets. Huge surpluses of bottles and knives built up and the people and government despaired.

Despite efforts by the island's Minister of Trade to revive the economy, the national income plunged. All seemed lost and the brave Minister, true to his country's ancient traditions, took the only honourable course. With a milk bottle in one hand and a table knife in the other he threw himself from Vitrasia's highest clifftop. As the unhappy politician sank to the seabed he plunged the knife into the ocean floor as his one, final act of defiance. It was in this way that Vitrasia discovered oil.

## THE GOVERNMENT OF VITRASIA

### Ministry of Development

1 Competitive bids are requested for the design and construction of a prototype oil rig for use in the Vitrasian Sea oil exploration project.

2 For reasons of national economy, the only materials to be used in this prototype are milk bottles and table knives.

3 The rig must stand on three legs. Three milk bottles should be used for this purpose.

4 The legs should be joined by three table knives.

5 The resulting structure should be able to support a fourth milk bottle which will be used to store oil pumped from the seabed. For this prototype the fourth bottle should contain water.

6 The whole structure should be able to withstand a full storm. The storm can be simulated by blowing with full force at the top bottle containing the water.

7 All competitors should be prepared to demonstrate their prototypes under full test conditions.

1 Divide into small groups and try to construct a rig using the materials described.

2 When you have a prototype, demonstrate it to your colleagues.

# Autotech and the electronic map

They said it couldn't be done. But by 1990 it was standard equipment in the top of the market Ashton XS 20 Saloon Car. The Electronic Map had arrived. For its inventor, John Lyle, Chairman of Autotech, the next question was how to reach a wider market with his brainchild. The answer was not long in coming. In 1992 Autotech unveiled to the motor trade a new, less expensive version of the original Automap.

1 Study the trade advertisement below.

2 Describe the features of the new product.

3 Make a list of the benefits of the electronic map for the motorist.

A small, innovative hi-tech company has to decide whether to stay small or expand

# Announcing the Autotech Automap Mk 2

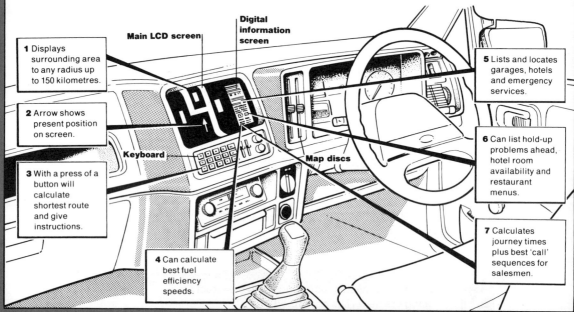

The Autotech Automap Mk 2 is probably the most important advance in automobile instrumentation in the last fifty years. Bringing the benefits of space technology to the ordinary motorist for the first time, it will present major competitive advantages to the manufacturers of middle range saloon cars. Not only will drivers of the future be able to watch themselves moving across an electronic map display, they will be able to identify the shortest route to a destination, cut fuel costs and even check the menu of a restaurant twenty miles ahead. At a basic list price of under £500, the Automap Mk 2 is no longer the rich man's toy. See it at next month's Auto Fair or call John Lyle on 02621–30004.

**Main LCD screen**

**Digital information screen**

**1** Displays surrounding area to any radius up to 150 kilometres.

**2** Arrow shows present position on screen.

**Keyboard**

**3** With a press of a button will calculate shortest route and give instructions.

**Map discs**

**4** Can calculate best fuel efficiency speeds.

**5** Lists and locates garages, hotels and emergency services.

**6** Can list hold-up problems ahead, hotel room availability and restaurant menus.

**7** Calculates journey times plus best 'call' sequences for salesmen.

**Autotech:** *High-tech partner of the motor industry*

48

# Small is beautiful

John Lyle is an engineer, cautious by training and cautious by nature. By allowing Autotech to grow slowly he had avoided many of the mistakes of his faster growing competitors. Autotech production had grown only as fast as his sales. Now, however, Lyle realized that Autotech was about to enter a much larger market. Success would have important implications for the company. Until such a time, Lyle saw no reason to change the habits of a lifetime.

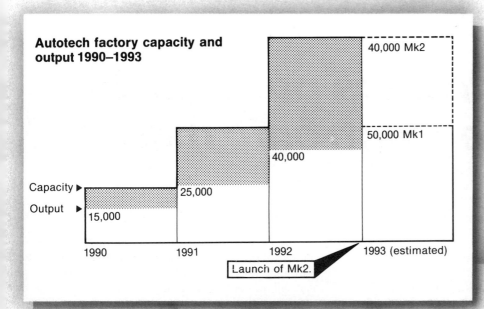

**Autotech factory capacity and output 1990–1993**

- 40,000 Mk2
- 50,000 Mk1
- 40,000
- 25,000
- 15,000

Capacity ▶
Output ▶

1990    1991    1992    1993 (estimated)

Launch of Mk2.

1 Study Autotech's production plans.

2 Describe Lyle's approach to factory expansion.

3 What are his plans for the Automap Mk 2 launch?

1 Study Autotech's policy document for the Mk 2.

2 What are its target customers for this product?

3 Describe Lyle's marketing plans.

```
To:      All department heads
From:    John Lyle
Subject: Automap Mk 2: Sales programme - HIGHLY CONFIDENTIAL
- - - - - - - - - - - - - - - - - - - - - - - - - - - - - - - - - -

At a meeting of the Automap Development Unit on July 25, the following
strategy was agreed for the launch of Automap Mk 2:

1  Because of present factory capacity limits, we will take a gradualist
   approach to sales of the new product. Expansion of capacity will take
   place only as we get a clear indication of future sales potential.

2  The market most likely to benefit from the product is the fleet
   market, eg car-hire companies, and so we shall approach the three
   major manufacturers of fleet models with a view to installing
   Automap Mk 2 as an optional extra.

3  We shall simultaneously approach the fleet companies themselves with
   a view to installing our equipment through them direct.

4  We are starting a low-key promotion campaign through the trade press
   with a view to establishing the product as a technical success in the
   first place rather than an immediate sales success.

5  Initial sales targets for 1993 are 40,000 units.
```

## . . . but big is sometimes necessary

Only a week after the Automap sales programme had been circulated among Autotech's management, the following article appeared in *Motoring Times*.

1 Read the article.

2 Describe
   a) Autotronics and
   b) the Navitron 1.

3 What are the implications of this news for Autotech?

Motoring Times, August 2nd

# Autotronics puts itself on the electronic map

The age of the driverless car came one step nearer yesterday with the surprise announcement from Autotronics, Britain's biggest autocomponents manufacturer, that it is soon to launch its answer to the Autotech Automap electronic map. Called the Navitron 1, it will sell at about £290 and do for the mass market what the Automap 1 did for the top of the market specialists. The Navitron 1 should bring the amazing see-where-you-are-see-where-you're-going benefits of the Automap to the ordinary motorist like you and me.

Of course the £290 price tag is what you would have to pay if you bought it from your local car accessories dealer. As a piece of original equipment built-in by the car makers the price could be much lower. And this, I suspect, is what Autotronics are aiming at. Users of the Automap in the XS 20 reckon that you can cut motoring costs by as much as 15% if you 'drive by the screen'. If the big fleet buyers could introduce such a machine into their vehicles, there is little doubt that the investment would pay off very quickly.

Insiders in the components industry believe that this is what Autotronics have in mind. Rumours suggest that the company is about to sign a major contract with one of the Big 3 car manufacturers. The likelihood is that the manufacturer will install the Navitron 1 in its best selling fleet car as a major competitive weapon in this cut throat sector of the market.

Although the Navitron would push up the price of the fleet car, it would probably recoup that cost easily over the typical 2.5 year life span of such a car.

A lot will depend on what unit price the manufacturer of Navitron can offer. The original Automap 1 sold at over £600 per unit. This price can only come down through improved design and longer. . .much longer. . . production runs.

Autotech itself has a lower priced version of the Automap in the pipeline but it could be that today's announcement from Autotronics has pipped Autotech at the electronic post.

# Autotech: which way now?

Three days and two sleepless nights later, John Lyle decided that the time had come to bite the bullet. Calling a series of meetings with his senior managers, he described the future as he saw it. 'I have the feeling,' he said wearily, 'that Autotech has reached some kind of watershed. We have the product, the problem is how the hell we are going to produce it in sufficient numbers to stop the competition swamping us?'

1 Study the supply structure of the car industry.

2 Who are the dominant manufacturers? Who are the dominant suppliers?

3 What is the basic problem facing Autotech?

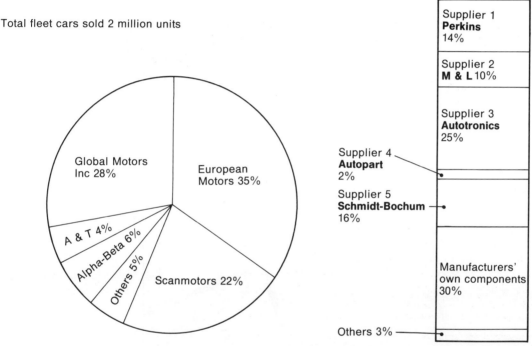

**European fleet car manufacturers and their electrical and electronic component suppliers**

Total fleet cars sold 2 million units

Global Motors Inc 28%

European Motors 35%

A & T 4%

Alpha-Beta 6%

Others 5%

Scanmotors 22%

Supplier 1 **Perkins** 14%

Supplier 2 **M & L** 10%

Supplier 3 **Autotronics** 25%

Supplier 4 **Autopart** 2%

Supplier 5 **Schmidt-Bochum** 16%

Manufacturers' own components 30%

Others 3%

1 Study the cost-benefit analysis below.

2 Calculate the cost savings per year for the user of Automap Mk 2.

3 How many years will it take for the Automap to pay back its price to the average user?

# International Road Research Institute

COST-BENEFIT STUDY OF AUTOMAP MK 2

*Sample:* Automap installed in 10 fleet cars over 6 month period. This period compared with previous 6 months.

Target maximum discount price for Automap: £490

---

*Basic information*

1 Average mileage p.a. of fleet car: 40,225 km

2 Average km.p.l. without Automap: 10.6 kilometres per litre

3 Average life of fleet car: 2.5 years

4 Average price per litre of fuel over test period: 50p

*Main findings*

1 Average reduction in total kilometres covered: 6%

2 Average reduction in fuel consumption per kilometre: 4%

3 Residual savings in time, etc: £10 per month

4 Depreciation rate of car equipped with Automap likely to decline.

# Action!

The agenda which arrived on the desks of Autotech's senior managers was short and to the point. There was no mistaking the urgency of the task before them. At the meeting sketched out before them they had to decide a completely new direction for Autotech.

## Internal memo

```
                    Management Planning Meeting


                           A G E N D A



        1  The potential market for Automap Mk 2.

        2  Outlet options:
             - standard equipment via car manufacturers.
             - optional extra via manufacturers.
             - accessories via parts dealers.
             - direct to fleet users.

        3  Production options:
             - own production.
             - license production via other producers.
             - joint venture with car manufacturer.
             - sub-contracted production either in UK or abroad.

        4  Present weaknesses and strengths of Autotech.

        5  Potential partners on marketing side.

        6  The question of expansion.

        7  Other business.
```

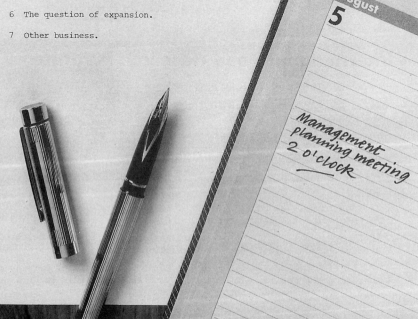

Management planning meeting 2 o'clock

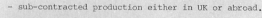
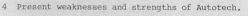

1 Divide into small specialist groups
   a) Sales and Marketing
   b) Production and
   c) John Lyle's management group.

2 The last group should call a meeting and follow the agenda below.

3 The meeting should decide a plan of action to ensure the best future for everyone at Autotech.

# The bottle experiment

Gordon Siu, an American scientist, once carried out an experiment using a bottle and two different kinds of insects. He took the bottle and laid it down horizontally with its closed base to a window and its open neck to the darker interior of his laboratory. He then introduced six bees and six common house flies into the bottle and sat back to observe.

The bees, considered to be the most intelligent creatures in the insect world, immediately flew towards the light and collided with the solid glass base of the bottle. Unable to see or understand the glass that separated them from the light, the bees swarmed and buzzed and threw themselves again and again against the invisible barrier. The flies on the other hand, considered to be the least intelligent creatures in the insect world, flew around the bottle in a casual and disorganized way with no obvious interest in the light. Within two minutes the flies had discovered the exit and were out into the air.

One hour later the six bees were lying dead, exhausted by their efforts, at the closed end of the bottle.

1 Discuss any message that the above story might have for business planning or corporate strategy.

2 Discuss ways in which your company could change its planning methods in the light of the experiment above.

# Please, Mr Banker?

Hunter-Benson is a merchant bank in the City of London. They specialize in organizing finance for businesses that wish to expand or take part in new ventures.

John Lyle of Autotech visits a bank to arrange finance for expansion.

Listen to the telephone call that Mark Hampshire, Hunter-Benson's motor industry specialist, received one morning from John Lyle, Chairman of Autotech and the inventor of the Automap Electronic Map.

1  What are John Lyle's general needs?

2  What are Mark Hampshire's needs at this stage?

1  Read the letter that Hampshire received the next day.

2  Identify Lyle's specific financial needs.

## AUTOTECH Ltd

Bromley Way
Beckenham
Kent KT9 4AD

Mr Mark Hampshire
Hunter-Benson Merchant Bank Ltd
12 City Wall
London EC1 2LA

15 September

Dear Mr Hampshire,

Following our recent telephone conversation, I should now like to outline our broad requirements over the coming 3 years.

Firstly, I should say that the new product I mentioned to you is a direct development of our highly successful Automap I electronic map. It has performed extremely well during testing and, we believe, has considerable commercial potential in the middle-range car market. To realise this potential, we shall have to radically expand our sales and production base. Our overall requirements can be summarised as follows:

1  To expand our production capacity from 90,000 to 400,000 units p.a.

2  To increase our present sales effort by £500,000 p.a.

3  To increase our R&D expenditure by £2m p.a.

Our initial estimates suggest a total capital injection of about £18m is required over the next two years. It is on this matter that we should appreciate your advice. I enclose the relevant financial statements for your perusal and look forward to meeting you personally on September 25.

Yours sincerely,

*John Lyle*

John Lyle, Chairman

# The banker and the industrialist

Ten days later John Lyle and his financial director at Autotech arrived at Hunter-Benson's plush London offices to present the Automap Mk2 and to answer questions about their present financial situation and their future needs.

1 Refer to Unit 10 and describe the commercial potential of the Automap Mk 2.

2 Study Autotech's Profit and Loss Account below and make sure you understand the different items.

3 Study Autotech's Balance Sheet on the next page and make sure you understand the different items.

4 Answer the questions below both financial statements.

## AUTOTECH Ltd — Profit and Loss Statements 1990–1992 (£000s)

| | 1992 | | 1991 | | 1990 | |
|---|---|---|---|---|---|---|
| **Turnover** | | 24,000 | | 15,000 | | 8,250 |
| Less: | | | | | | |
| **Cost of sales** | | | | | | |
| Materials | 6,000 | | 3,500 | | 1,500 | |
| Labour | 4,000 | | 3,000 | | 2,200 | |
| Factory Overheads (Inc. Deprcn) | 6,000 | | 4,000 | | 3,000 | |
| | 16,000 | | 10,500 | | 6,700 | |
| **Gross profit** | | 8,000 | | 4,500 | | 1,550 |
| Distribution costs | 531 | | 298 | | 50 | |
| Head office | | | | | | |
| Admin. costs | 580 | | 380 | | 150 | |
| R & D | 2,374 | | 989 | | 976 | |
| Depreciation of non-manufacturing assets | 200 | | 200 | | 200 | |
| Interest payable | 579 | | 420 | | 48 | |
| | 4,264 | | 2,287 | | 1,424 | |
| **Net profit before tax** | | 3,736 | | 2,213 | | 126 |
| Corporation tax @ 35% | | 1,307.6 | | 774.5 | | 44.1 |
| **Net profit after tax** | | 2,428.4 | | 1,438.5 | | 81.9 |
| **Retained profit b/f** | | 1,274.1 | | 135.6 | | 73.7 |
| **Dividends payable** | | 500 | | 300 | | 20 |
| **Retained profits c/f** | | 3,202.5 | | 1,274.1 | | 135.6 |

1 Study the profit and loss account over the years 1990–1992.

2 What happened to
   a) turnover,
   b) ratio of labour to turnover,
   c) R and D expenditure,
   d) profit before tax as a proportion of turnover,
   e) interest payments,
   f) payments of dividends?

3 Tell the story of the company's operations over the past three years in words which a layman could understand.

# AUTOTECH Ltd — Balance Sheet Summaries 1990–1992 (£000s)

| | 1992 | | 1991 | | 1990 | |
|---|---|---|---|---|---|---|
| **Fixed assets** (Net written down value) | | | | | | |
| Land and buildings | 4,500 | | 3,500 | | 1,305.8 | |
| Plant and machinery | 8,500 | | 5,000 | | 3,000 | |
| Vehicles | 300 | | 200 | | 100 | |
| | | 13,300 | | 8,700 | | 4,405.8 |
| **Current assets** | | | | | | |
| Stock and work in progress | 2,300 | | 1,250 | | 687.5 | |
| Debtors | 3,000 | | 1,300 | | 700 | |
| Cash in bank | 1,400 | | 500 | | 200 | |
| | 6,700 | | 3,050 | | 1,587.5 | |
| Less: | | | | | | |
| **Current liabilities** | | | | | | |
| Creditors | 2,100 | | 1,000 | | 600 | |
| Accruals | 772.4 | | 99.2 | | 96.3 | |
| Taxation | 1,307.6 | | 774.5 | | 44.1 | |
| | 4,180 | 2,520 | 1,873.7 | 1,176.3 | 740.4 | 847.1 |
| **Capital employed** (net assets) | | 15,820 | | 9,876.3 | | 5,252.9 |
| Share capital – £1 Ordinary shares fully paid up | 8,000 | | 5,276.3 | | 4,717.3 | |
| Share premium | 1,000 | | 800 | | Nil | |
| Retained profits | 3,202.5 | | 1,274.1 | | 135.6 | |
| **Shareholders' funds** | | 12,202.5 | | 7,350.4 | | 4,852.9 |
| Long-term loans | | 3,617.5 | | 2,525.9 | | 400 |
| **Balance sheet total** | | 15,820 | | 9,876.3 | | 5,252.9 |

1 Calculate the following ratios:
  a) return on capital over 3 years;
  b) debt/equity ratio over 3 years;
  c) changes in Debtors/Creditors ratio over 3 years;
  d) changes in the current ratio over 3 years;
  e) earnings per share 1990–1992.

2 Decide what advice you would give Lyle about the £18m extra finance.

# Meeting!

John Lyle and his colleagues were expecting some tough talking at the bank and were ready with their arguments. They expected few problems with their accounts over the last three years but they knew that those accounts were based on one product with a captive market.

At the moment they had not signed any contract with a car manufacturer or accessories chain for their Automap Mk 2. Even so, if they could convince the bank to back them, their chances in the market would be excellent. Lyle reckoned that if he could get the Automap accepted by one of the Big 3 he could move over

300,000 Mk 2s in the first year. Even if he could only sell to a dealer chain he estimated a first year sales of 100,000. If he pitched the price at £250 per unit he could expect a turnover of £75m to £100m, in addition to the continuing sales of the Mk 1.

There were many other points to consider. But that's what bankers were for, wasn't it? He knew what he wanted. They had to tell him how he could get it.

Meanwhile Mark Hampshire and his colleagues had been doing their homework. The various options they saw open to Autotech were as follows:

## Hunter-Benson Merchant Bank

1   Arrange a roll-over loan secured against assets for a period of, say, 5 years.

2   Raise the necessary funds in the Eurobond market.

3   Study the possibility of a joint venture with one of the automobile majors with manufacturing facilities separate from Autotech's present factory.

4   Arrange a private sale of shares to an automobile major at a premium that would reflect the potential of the new invention.

5   Float a major portion of Autotech's shares on the stock exchange.

6   Sell the new product as a licence to an automobile major.

1 Divide into two groups representing Autotech and Hunter-Benson Bank.

2 Each group should familiarize itself with the information and issues relevant to the situation and needs.

3 The Autotech Group should now present
   a) the technical aspects of Automap,
   b) its market potential, and
   c) their financial needs to exploit this potential.

4 The Hunter-Benson Group should question Autotech about
   a) the commercial and technical aspects of Automap,
   b) their financial statements.

   They should then present the options open to Autotech.

5 With the help of Hunter-Benson, Autotech should now decide the appropriate strategy for raising the necessary capital.

57

# Agrichem International

Agrichem International is a major producer of herbicides and pesticides with companies and distributors around the world. Although controlled centrally from its head office outside Brussels, Agrichem relies heavily upon its system of agents and distributors abroad.

1 Listen to the telephone call received early one morning at Agrichem's head office.

2 Identify the complaints of Sr Sanchez.

3 Identify any possible causes of the problems.

Immediately after the call, Robert Mathison called in Bill Thompson, Sales Director for Ecuador and asked him to brief him on the current situation in that country.

1 Study the map below.

2 Describe the range of Agrichem products sold in Ecuador and their distribution channels.

3 Describe Ecuador's overall current export situation.

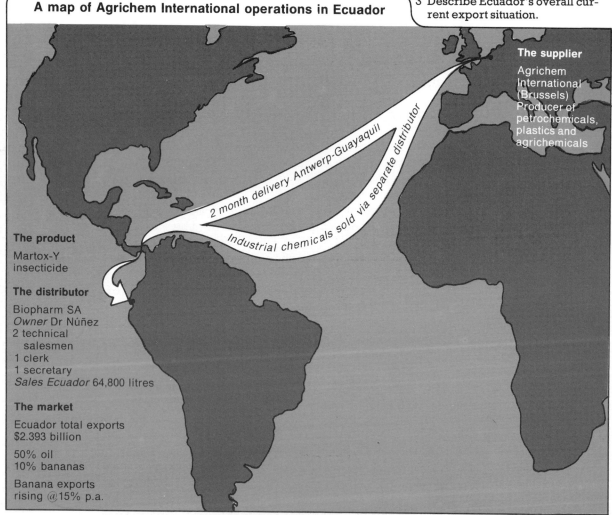

**A map of Agrichem International operations in Ecuador**

2 month delivery Antwerp-Guayaquil

Industrial chemicals sold via separate distributor

**The supplier**

Agrichem International (Brussels) Producer of petrochemicals, plastics and agrichemicals

**The product**

Martox-Y insecticide

**The distributor**

Biopharm SA
*Owner* Dr Núñez
2 technical salesmen
1 clerk
1 secretary
*Sales Ecuador* 64,800 litres

**The market**

Ecuador total exports $2.393 billion

50% oil
10% bananas

Banana exports rising @ 15% p.a.

# The Ecuador File

The picture in Ecuador became clearer when Thompson introduced his latest analysis of Biopharm's performance over the last four years.

1 Study the information below.

2 Describe the changing pattern of banana production and exports in Ecuador over recent years.

3 Compare Biopharm's penetration of this market with similar distributors in other South American countries.

# AGRICHEM INTERNATIONAL B.V.

South America File

ECUADOR

Distributor: Biopharm SA (Dr Emilio Núñez)

## 1 Ecuador: Sales of Martox-Y insecticide

| Year | Total litres | Planted hectares (bananas) | | Total area | Litres per hectare | Litres per hectare (average, S. Amer.) |
| | | Gros Michel bananas | Cavendish bananas | | | |
|---|---|---|---|---|---|---|
| 1985 | 59,400 | 44,000 | 29,000 | 73,000 | 0.86 | 2.9 |
| 1986 | 60,200 | 30,000 | 41,000 | 71,000 | 0.90 | 3.1 |
| 1987 | 59,400 | 19,000 | 47,000 | 66,000 | 0.96 | 3.6 |
| 1988 | 64,800 | 8,000 | 58,000 | 66,000 | 1.05 | 3.9 |

*All but 5% of banana crop is exported

## 2 Ecuador: Exports of bananas 1985-88

| | 1985 | 1986 | 1987 | 1988 | % change |
|---|---|---|---|---|---|
| Bananas | 138.3 | 171.6 | 200.1 | 237.1 | ? |
| Total exports | 1191.6 | 1493.8 | 2172.7 | 2393.6 | ? |

# Goodbye Dr Núñez. Hello Sr . . . ?

The decision to buy themselves out of the contract with Biopharm was made one week after the call from Frutas Internacionales. The problem now was to replace them with an aggressive, effective distributor who would realise the full potential of Martox Y and any future AI products. Bill Thompson had a number of contacts in Ecuador and he drew up a short list of contenders for the new distributorship.

1 Listen to Mathison and Thompson discussing the qualities they need in a new distributor.

2 Decide which qualities you think are most important.

3 Study the short list below.

---

Company: Grunwald SA

Location: Guayaquil & Quito

Turnover: $25m

Established: 1934

Owners: 30% German Chemical Company
70% Ecuadorian
(Sr Steinbach)

Grunwald is a very real contender. Steinbach has been in Ecuador for many years and knows the agrichemical market like the back of his hand. As well as being distributor for the German company, Grunwald also distributes for a major Swiss concern. Main products - weedkillers, herbicides and insecticides. Could be a conflict of interest here. Steinbach is not prepared to give up any of existing distributorships but very interested in Martox. Excellent connections and distribution system. Modern, professional management.

---

Company: Mercator SA

Location: San José & Quito

Turnover: $8.5m

Established: 1950

Owners: Sr López & family

Mercator are one of the major banana growers in Ecuador and they consume 15,000 litres of Martox p.a. Sr López is also a major political figure and has excellent connections in banana industry. Management is very good and finance is sound. Only distribution network is from plantations to ports. No experience in selling chemicals or in marketing and promoting products inside Ecuador. Also banana exports would always be main concern. Even so, Sr López is very interested in diversifying out of bananas and sees distributorship as a major opportunity for achieving this.

---

Company: Royce-Martínez SA

Location: Quito

Turnover: $3.5m

Established: 1981

Owners: Brian Royce and wife (née Martínez)

Brian Royce emigrated to Colombia in 1968. He moved to Ecuador in 1975 as head of a plastics company. Met his wife there and married in 79. She has money and they set up own plastics company in 1981. Rapid growth in turnover since then. Royce is very experienced plastics specialist but knows nothing of agrochemicals. Became AI's distributor for industrial chemicals 18 months ago and that business is doing very well. Very keen to expand and wants to get into agrochemicals because he believes Ecuador is set for 'explosive growth' in this area. Has a well-developed distribution system for AI industrial chemicals.

---

Hold a meeting with your colleagues to discuss the advantages and disadvantages of the potential new distributors above. Decide to whom you will offer the contract and justify your choice.

# Negotiation!

One month later Thompson was on the plane to Quito. In his brief-case he carried a position paper drawn up with Mathison as a basis for negotiations with the new distributor. Meanwhile in Quito the new distributor was working out his own position for the coming negotiations.

1 Divide into two groups: Agrichem Group and the new distributor.

2 Agrichem Group should study position paper 1. Discuss it and justify its clauses to each other.

3 The new distributor should study position paper 2 on page 62. Discuss it and work out your tactics for the negotiations.

**Group 1**

# AGRICHEM INTERNATIONAL B.V.

Position paper for negotiations with new distributor

C O N F I D E N T I A L

1 An effective distributor in Ecuador should be able to sell up to 170,000 litres of Martox-Y p.a.

2 In the first year, we would expect an opening stock of 40,000 litres.

3 Our price F.O.B. is $3.00 per litre. Distributor could charge up to $7.00. Cost of C.I.F. is 18 cents, so effective price per litre is $3.18.

4 Typical credit period in our business is 120 days.

5 We require exclusive distributorships in agrochemical products.

6 We should retain the option to appoint other distributors for other products.

7 New distributor should set up a viable sales unit within 6 months.

8 The sales unit should consist of:

    a) 1 general manager
    b) 1 accountant
    c) 1 graduate technician for product registration
    d) 4 indigenous technical salesmen
    e) 3 office staff

9 We can offer one of our top people as G.M. for 3 years and will pay 50% of his salary and relocation expenses for a period of 1 year.

10 If the volume target in (1) above is not reached in two years, we retain the right to cancel the contract immediately.

11 6-monthly review periods should be built into the contract and both sides should have the right to cancel the contract with 6 months notice.

**Group 2**

Position paper for negotiations with Agrichem International

Confidential

1 Present sales of AI Martox-Y are 64,800 litres per annum.

2 Probable sales price of Martox-Y is $6.00 per litre. Above that there would be considerable price resistance. Price could fall to $5.00.

3 Typical payment period in Ecuador is 160-240 days. In addition to this, there will be a 60-day period of goods in transit from Rotterdam to Guayaquil. If Agrichem invoice us 60 days before we receive stock, we would have considerable cash-flow difficulties.

4 We require therefore, either 8 months credit for first 3 years or 20% of initial starting capital for the project.

5 Agrichem should supply:

a) 1 resident technical manager for the first year at their expense.

b) 1 general manager for 3 years, and should bear half the cost.

6 Contract to run for 3 years and to be renewed each year for an identical period.

7 We require first option on any other Agrichem products.

8 We must retain an option to market other manufacturers' products as long as they are non-competing.

9 Additional discount to be given on sales above agreed target as an incentive.

| Capital needed (Year 1) | $000 |
|---|---|
| Opening stock (15,000 litres) | 48 |
| Debtors | 150 |
| Marketing | 50 |
| Admin | 30 |
| Contingency | 25 |
| Total | 303 |

| Rough profit/loss account (Year 1) | $000 | |
|---|---|---|
| Sales (90,000 litres) | 540 | |
| Less cost of product (C.I.F.) | 288 | |
| Gross margin | | 252 |
| Less: | | |
| Sales expenses | 73 | |
| Advertising | 60 | |
| Admin | 10 | |
| Distribution | 10 | |
| Bad debts | 22.5 | |
| Cost of trials & govt licences | 20 | |
| Total | | 195 |
| Net contribution to overheads and profits | | 56.5 |

1 As Agrichem, outline your initial negotiating position.

2 As the new distributor outline your initial position.

3 Negotiate with each other to a successful conclusion.

1 As Agrichem's Bill Thompson, fill in the final decisions grid below.

2 Telephone Robert Mathison in Brussels and inform him of the outcome.

FINAL AGREEMENT between AGRICHEM and THE NEW DISTRIBUTOR

| | |
|---|---|
| Sales targets, Year 1 | Selling price |
| Sales targets, Year 2 | Buying price |
| Sales targets, Year 3 | Discounts ? |
| Credit terms (days) | Opening stock |
| Capital injection ? | Personnel |
| Other | Contract period and renewal |

## REPORT

1 Write a telex from Bill Thompson back to Robert Mathison in Brussels telling him about the outcome of your negotiations with the new distributor.

2 As the new distributor write a formal letter confirming the main points reached in your discussions with Thompson to Agrichem's Head Office in Brussels.

3 Write a brief informal letter to the new distributor thanking them for their hospitality and looking forward to years of collaboration.

# Our man in Nam Doa

A Swedish project in the Far East goes wrong when a key man goes missing.

The telex in Jan Berling's in-tray on Monday morning was short and to the point.

1 Study the telex.

2 Report its contents in spoken English.

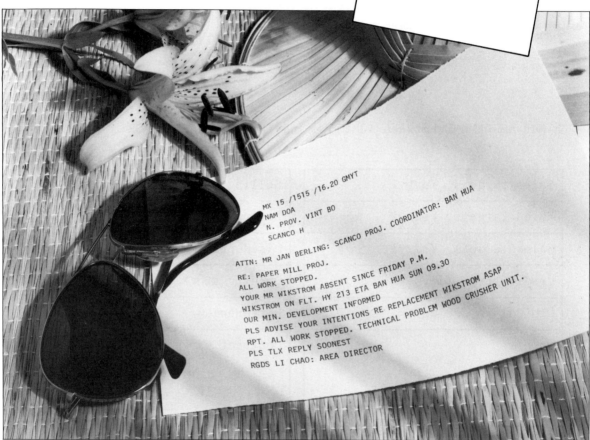

```
MX 15 /1515 /16.20 GMYT
NAM DOA
  N. PROV. VINT BO
  SCANCO H

ATTN: MR JAN BERLING: SCANCO PROJ. COORDINATOR: BAN HUA
RE: PAPER MILL PROJ.
ALL WORK STOPPED.
YOUR MR WIKSTROM ABSENT SINCE FRIDAY P.M.
WIKSTROM ON FLT. HY 213 ETA BAN HUA SUN 09.30
OUR MIN. DEVELOPMENT INFORMED
PLS ADVISE YOUR INTENTIONS RE REPLACEMENT WIKSTROM ASAP
RPT. ALL WORK STOPPED. TECHNICAL PROBLEM WOOD CRUSHER UNIT.
PLS TLX REPLY SOONEST
RGDS LI CHAO: AREA DIRECTOR
```

## Background

The Nam Doa Paper Mill is a prestige project for Scanco AB, one of Sweden's leading producers of specialized machinery for paper mills. Not only is it a very profitable project, it is also Scanco's first major overseas contract. For this reason Scanco sent Jan Berling one of their best managers to the capital Ban Hua. His job was to liaise with the Ministry of Development and to oversee the supplies of plant and equipment from the port at Ban Hua to the remote Nam Doa site 500 miles to the north. In the first year the project went well. It was when the first machinery was being installed that things began to go wrong. The installation needed highly specialized technical personnel from Sweden under a Technical Liaison Manager. The first man in this job returned to Sweden after an incident at an embassy party. This man's replacement was Nils Wikström, a much quieter and more dependable person. Wikström agreed to go out to Nam Doa as long as his family could join him there. It seemed a strange request to Berling but in the end he agreed. After all, it was most unlikely that a family man like Wikström would cause any problems with the diplomatic corps!

# A note from Wikström

Jan Berling acted quickly. He first of all contacted the hostel where Wikström's family had been staying temporarily while he looked for accommodation for them in Nam Doa. They were not there. He then checked the main hotels in Ban Hua. No one had heard of a Mr Wikström. Finally he checked the airport. An SAS flight had left for Stockholm on Sunday lunch time. As he put down the phone his secretary came in with an envelope marked *Urgent*. In the envelope was the document below.

1 Study the document.
2 Present and explain the formal clauses in the document.
3 Present and interpret Wikström's handwritten comments.

---

# SCANCO AB

*Three weeks in this place would be too much!*

*The German site manager is on 3 × my salary*

Conditions of employment for all staff on Far East assignments

1· Unless otherwise stated, assignments will be of (three years) duration.

2 A (50%) supplement of Swedish gross salary shall be paid monthly into the employee's bank account in Sweden.

*You call this an allowance when 20 cigs cost Kr 30 & whisky Kr 140?*

3 A messing allowance of (Kr 200) per day will be paid while the employee is living away from his overseas home.

*when do I get time for this?*

4 The employee shall initially travel to the assignment alone and will be responsible for arranging family accommodation if his family intends to join him.

5 Standard company accommodation will be provided for single employees.

6 A schooling allowance of 50% of school fees will be paid for children between the ages of 4-15.

*which schools? where? The fees in the diplomatic schools are ½ my annual home salary!*

7 In addition to the starting and terminating journeys, one return air fare for the family will be paid each year to the domicile in Sweden.

8 Full medical insurance will be provided for the employee and his family.

*Is this to cover my funeral expenses?*

9 A (terminal) gratuity of 20% of gross salary over the period of the assignment will be paid on completion of the full period of the assignment.

10 The employee shall be responsible for repatriating himself and his family if for any reason he fails to fulfil the assignment without the agreement of the company.

*we'll see about this when I reach Stockholm!*

# Berling calls the Ministry and checks the files

Unable to clarify the situation, Berling decided to take the bull by the horns and called his contact at the Ministry of Development.

1 Listen to the conversation between Berling and the Ministry.
2 Report its contents to your colleagues.
3 Interpret the events so far.

While Berling was on the phone to the Ministry, his secretary looked up the file on Nils Wikström. In the file she found the original notification from the Personnel Division in Stockholm of Wikström's appointment.

1 Study the letter below.
2 Report its contents to your colleagues.
3 Interpret its contents in the light of recent events.

## SCANCO AB

Jan Berling                                          August 15
Project Coordinator
Scanco AB
Ban Hua


Dear Jan,

You will be glad to hear that we have selected a replacement for Björn Jacobson as Technical Liaison Manager at Nam Doa. His name is Nils Wikström and he's very different from Jacobson. He seems a very sensitive sort of man and I am sure he will get on better with the locals down there, not to mention the embassy staff! Nils is married with one kid and he is one of our top technical people at the Norköpping factory.

He is rather a quiet sort of guy, but once you get to know him, you'll see how good he is at his job. He's a bit of a perfectionist but that's exactly what we need to get the standards. He is the man who solved the computerisation problem on the pulping units. One of his interests is oriental art, so he should get on well in your part of the world. You certainly won't have any of the bar-room problems you had with Jacobson.

Wikström has put one condition on his acceptance of the post and that is that his wife and child can join him after the regulation 3 months. As long as you can arrange accommodation, we see no reason why they cannot accompany him. His wife, by the way, is a very confident lady with a big interest in Third World development. This is one of the reasons why she wants to come out with him. We have warned her about the hardships but she says she doesn't mind.

Incidentally, none of them has been on an overseas assignment before, so can you give them as much help as possible?

I look forward to seeing you on your next leave,

Gunnar

# Another telex: Berling prepares for a very important meeting

From the files a clearer picture began to emerge of Nils Wikström and the problems at Nam Doa. Even so, the immediate need was to replace Wikström as soon as possible. Once again, however, Berling was overtaken by events.

1 Study the telex which arrived before Berling could send his message to Stockholm.

2 Present its contents and interpret its implications for Jan Berling.

```
LSY / STCKHM / 23335 / 10.45 :30 GMT

SCANCO SH

ATTN: BERLING  SCANCO  BAN HUA


WIKSTROM ARRIVED HERE THIS A.M. IN STATE SEVERE DEPRESSION.
NOW UNDER SEDATION.

INDICATES LACK OF SUPPORT CAUSED BREAKDOWN OF MORALE AND COMMUNICATION
PROBLEMS WITH LOCAL PERSONNEL A PARTICULAR PROBLEM AREA.

ALSO ROW WITH WIFE INDICATED. WHERE IS SHE NOW?

WIKSTROM HAS OFFERED RESIGNATION FROM SCANCO.

TLX RECEIVED FROM MIN. DEV. BAN HUA RE NAM DOA PROJECT. WANT CLARIFICATION
STATE OF PROJECT EARLIEST PLUS REPLACEMENT WIKSTROM.

STRONG HINT PENALTIES OR CANCELLATION.

AM FLYING OUT THIS P.M. ETA BAN HUA 23.30 TUES.

TECHNICIAN ACCOMPANYING.

LARS ARLBJORG  MAN. DIRECTOR.
```

1 Discuss the problem and its causes using the notes that Berling made while he waited for his Managing Director to arrive.

2 Prepare some recommendations to avoid the problems in the future.

1. RECRUITMENT
2. ACCLIMATISATION
3. CONDITIONS
4. TRAINING ROLE
5. ROLE OF PROJ. CO-ORDINATOR
6. WIKSTRÖM'S WIFE
7. RECOMMENDATIONS

## REPORT

1 Write a formal report to the Scanco Board analyzing the problems in Nam Doa and making recommendations for the future.

2 Write a letter of apology to the Ministry of Development and outline the measures you are taking to ensure the situation is not repeated.

# Sea link

Grunland and Latonia have been separated since the Ice Age by a narrow stretch of water only 30 kilometres wide. The Western Channel used to protect both countries from each other's territorial ambitions. Today it is simply an obstacle to greater trade between the two countries.

Two countries must decide the best way to close the gap that has separated them for centuries.

1 Study the news report about the proposed link.

2 Identify the main commercial precondition for any bid.

3 List some of the other factors which could affect any choice of bids.

## HOME NEWS

# Go-ahead for cross-channel link

*from our Home Affairs Correspondent* Tim Underwood

IN A JOINT DECLARATION issued by the governments of Grunland and Latonia last night, formal approval was given for the construction of a fixed link to join the two countries across the Western Channel. This long awaited and historic declaration caused a flurry of commercial activity on both sides of the channel. The various consortia who have been waiting in the wings for months all called press conferences to announce their various proposals for the link-up.

The declaration made it clear that no government funds would be available for the project and that the selected proposal must be self-financing. In addition to this, it is likely that the governments will judge each bid on a variety of other criteria. Safety and security will be important considerations in their assessment. So too will be the impact on unemployment in the areas close to the proposed link. One of the major factors will be the attitudes of different interest groups to any proposal. For example, Grunland National Railways would make it difficult for the Grunland government to accept any proposal that did not include a rail-link in its plans. The Latonian Ferry Operators group which now controls the existing ferry routes across the channel are also expected to influence any decision. The governments will also be interested in the impact that the project will have on employment. In Grunland for example, 15% of the workforce is unemployed. A labour intensive dash to a fixed link would certainly help the government's prospects of re-election especially if that fixed link could be opened a few weeks before the next election.

Last night, such factors were temporarily forgotten amongst the popping of champagne corks and the toasting of new friends . . .

# The problem

The Western Channel is one of the busiest waterways in the world. It is also renowned for its bad weather conditions and its difficult geology.

1 Study the map below.
2 List the problems that the fixed link will face.
3 Assess the commercial potential of a fixed link.

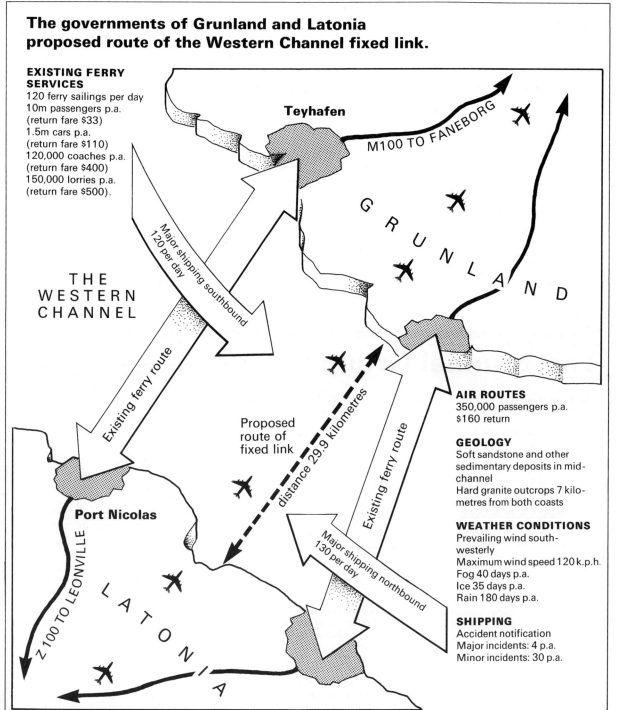

**The governments of Grunland and Latonia proposed route of the Western Channel fixed link.**

**EXISTING FERRY SERVICES**
120 ferry sailings per day
10m passengers p.a.
(return fare $33)
1.5m cars p.a.
(return fare $110)
120,000 coaches p.a.
(return fare $400)
150,000 lorries p.a.
(return fare $500).

Teyhafen

M100 TO FANEBORG

G R U N L A N D

THE WESTERN CHANNEL

Major shipping southbound 120 per day

Existing ferry route

Proposed route of fixed link

distance 29.9 kilometres

Existing ferry route

Major shipping northbound 130 per day

Port Nicolas

Z100 TO LEONVILLE

L A T O N I A

**AIR ROUTES**
350,000 passengers p.a.
$160 return

**GEOLOGY**
Soft sandstone and other sedimentary deposits in mid-channel
Hard granite outcrops 7 kilometres from both coasts

**WEATHER CONDITIONS**
Prevailing wind south-westerly
Maximum wind speed 120 k.p.h.
Fog 40 days p.a.
Ice 35 days p.a.
Rain 180 days p.a.

**SHIPPING**
Accident notification
Major incidents: 4 p.a.
Minor incidents: 30 p.a.

## The bids

At press conferences held in the capitals of both countries the four consortia in the bid to build the Channel link presented their projects.

1 Compare the technical aspects of the four proposals and explain how they would overcome the difficulties of trans-channel transportation.
2 Compare the economic advantages and disadvantages of each project.

# The Bridge Consortium

'The fastest, most elegant solution to bridging that gap'...
*The Architect*

- This is a direct road link between both countries
- Drivers and passengers do not have to leave vehicles
- No disruption due to strikes, tunnel blockages
- Very low running costs
- No expensive ventilating costs
- Proven design – similar bridges already in operation

6 lane motorway suspended in an aerodynamic tube

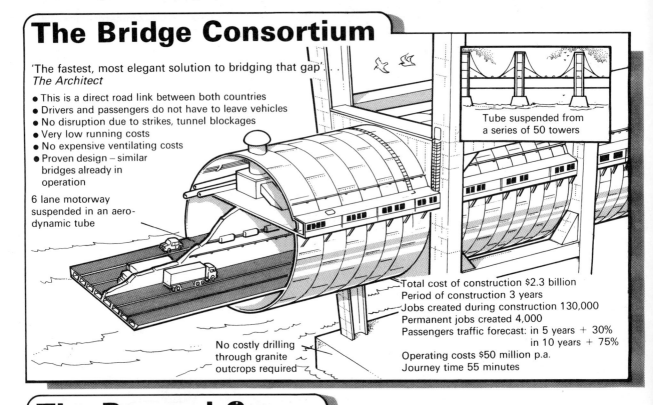

Tube suspended from a series of 50 towers

No costly drilling through granite outcrops required

Total cost of construction $2.3 billion
Period of construction 3 years
Jobs created during construction 130,000
Permanent jobs created 4,000
Passengers traffic forecast: in 5 years + 30%
                      in 10 years + 75%
Operating costs $50 million p.a.
Journey time 55 minutes

# The Brunnel Group

'The Brunnel concept – part bridge, part tunnel – offers the speed and elegance of a bridge with the safety and security of a tunnel'... *The Environmental Times*

bridge over granite outcrops to islands

islands providing access to tunnels

island customs and free port facilities avoiding congestion at land terminals

road tunnel

central channel for shipping

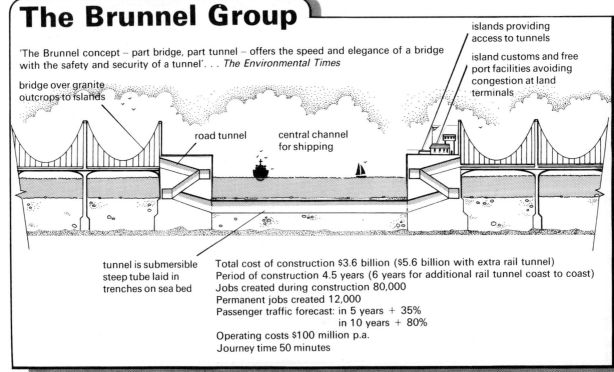

tunnel is submersible steep tube laid in trenches on sea bed

Total cost of construction $3.6 billion ($5.6 billion with extra rail tunnel)
Period of construction 4.5 years (6 years for additional rail tunnel coast to coast)
Jobs created during construction 80,000
Permanent jobs created 12,000
Passenger traffic forecast: in 5 years + 35%
                      in 10 years + 80%
Operating costs $100 million p.a.
Journey time 50 minutes

# The Tunnel Group

'It is the only scheme that is technically and financially viable'...
*International Construction Journal*

- The simplest and most troublefree solution
- Twin-bore tunnel with railway shuttle service every 5 minutes
- Tunnel bored under the seabed
- No delays due to bad weather
- Drivers and passengers transfer to railway carriages and can relax, watch films and eat in restaurant during journey

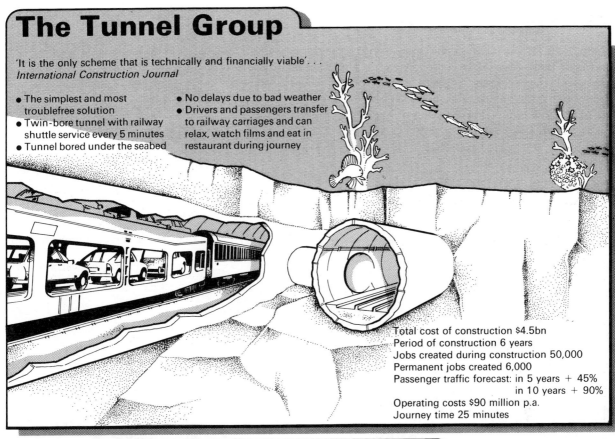

Total cost of construction $4.5bn
Period of construction 6 years
Jobs created during construction 50,000
Permanent jobs created 6,000
Passenger traffic forecast: in 5 years + 45%
in 10 years + 90%
Operating costs $90 million p.a.
Journey time 25 minutes

# The Super-ferry Consortium

'The link already exists. In 5 years time the new, super ferries will provide a flexible, proven service at half the present cost to users'... *The Shipping Monitor*

- The new super ferries will double the capacity on existing routes
- Fares will fall by 50%
- Improved comfort and facilities
- Can operate in almost all weather conditions
- All other consortia's passenger forecasts are optimistic
- Existing ferry companies employ 40,000 people
- All these jobs at risk from a fixed link

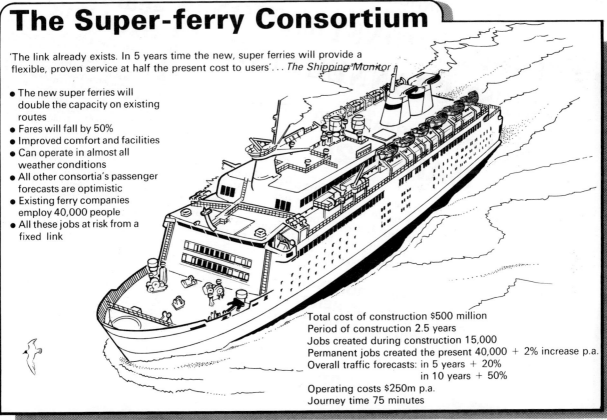

Total cost of construction $500 million
Period of construction 2.5 years
Jobs created during construction 15,000
Permanent jobs created the present 40,000 + 2% increase p.a.
Overall traffic forecasts: in 5 years + 20%
in 10 years + 50%
Operating costs $250m p.a.
Journey time 75 minutes

## An historic opportunity

Each of the consortia knew that they would have to argue their cases on two levels. Firstly, there was the purely commercial and economic basis. Secondly, there was the political basis. Although both governments firmly denied that political factors would influence their final decision, only the politically naive thought that the governments were doing this only to help Big Business get bigger.

1  Study the four documents.
2  List the factors which will influence the governments of Grunland and Latonia.

Consider the options facing the two governments and select the option that will best satisfy the following criteria:
a) commercial criteria
b) technical and other non-commercial criteria
c) economic and political criteria.

# Residents of Latonia demand public enquiry

The recent announcement of the Western Channel project caused a fierce reaction last night at a public meeting of local residents. The overall objection was the lack of consultation in an area which is bound to be affected by the new link. More specifically, residents were angry about the possible job losses that may come from the end of the ferry industry which is the mainstay of the local economy. They were also concerned about the disruption and damage to the local environment caused by any new mainland terminals. Councillor Paul Houseman who himself owns 1000 hectares of land on the site of one of the proposed terminals said that the new link would destroy the local community, wild life and thousands of acres of prime agricultural land. Other objectors spoke of the disgraceful and outrageous behaviour of central government and ...

### GRUNLAND NATIONAL PARTY

# PROTEST DEMONSTRATION AGAINST CHANNEL LINK

## CONSTITUTION SQUARE FANEBORG

# MARCH 20

The stretch of water that has separated this country from the mainland throughout our history is what made this country unique. We are an island race and our way of life, our laws and our constitution are the product of the security and separation given to us by nature. A fixed link will be not only unnatural, it will be the beginning of the end of this nation.

**FIGHT THE PROPOSALS!**
**FIGHT FOR YOUR HERITAGE!**
**FIGHT THE CHANNEL LINK!**

Send coupon to HE Holida...

## Rabies scare over fixed link

A hundred years of strict medical and customs regulations to stop rabies entering this country may come to nothing if a Channel Fixed Link is built according to a report out today by the Grunland Medical Council. The disease which is endemic in Latonia could endanger both the human and animal populations of this country. The report suggests that affected animals could cross by bridge or tunnel and enter Grunland with little chance of detection. Only drastic and expensive prevention measures would

Do you ever get that sinking, spinning, smothering feeling when you travel on the underground? Well, according to a survey by Dr Alan Gill of the Latonian Institute of Psychology, 30% of us suffer some form of psychological reaction when travelling in enclosed spaces. His tests show that these reactions can result in severe behavioural disturbances in 10% of those affected. Of course Dr Gill is not concerned particularly about the underground. He is much more worried about drivers travelling across the proposed fixed link. He points out that no one has ever tested driving behaviour in a tunnel as long as 30 miles. Nor for that matter does anyone know what will happen in a suspended tube when the wind begin to blow. Dr Gill is adamant. Psychological testing is as important for any of

# The tower

### The continuing history of Vitrasia

The small and oil rich country of Vitrasia has decided to build a memorial tower to its ex-Minister of Trade who gave his life in the search for oil. Although now fabulously rich once more, Vitracia remembers the days of economic hardship and is determined to use its present resources efficiently. Thus although the new commemorative tower should be as high as possible, the chosen contractor will have to demonstrate that he will use less bricks than any of his competitors. All in all, candidates for the contract will be selected according to three factors:

a) The height of the tower
b) The number of bricks used
c) The speed of erection.

Study the advertisement that appeared in the Times of Vitrasia:

## THE GOVERNMENT OF VITRASIA

1 **Competitive bids are requested for the building of a commemorative tower to our ex-Minister of Trade.**

2 **The tower should be constructed solely from our major new manufactured product namely, standard Lego bricks.**

3 **The tower can be of any design but must be freestanding and be stable enough to be measured.**

4 **The tower must be as high as possible. The higher the tower, the more marks will be awarded.**

5 **The tower should consist of as few bricks as possible. The fewer bricks used the more marks that will be awarded.**

6 **The tower should be constructed as quickly as possible. The faster it is constructed the more marks that will be awarded.**

1 Divide into small groups and experiment with the bricks provided.

2 Remember your tower will be measured against the three factors above.

3 When you are ready, present and demonstrate your prototype towers.

# Chun and the desktop computer

**UNIT 15**

A Korean typewriter manufacturer finds that his new computer needs a different marketing structure.

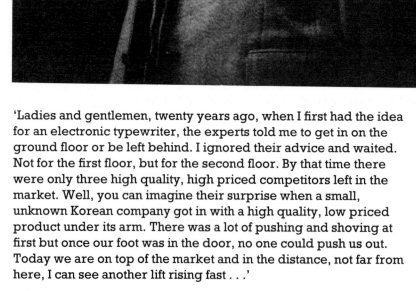

'Ladies and gentlemen, twenty years ago, when I first had the idea for an electronic typewriter, the experts told me to get in on the ground floor or be left behind. I ignored their advice and waited. Not for the first floor, but for the second floor. By that time there were only three high quality, high priced competitors left in the market. Well, you can imagine their surprise when a small, unknown Korean company got in with a high quality, low priced product under its arm. There was a lot of pushing and shoving at first but once our foot was in the door, no one could push us out. Today we are on top of the market and in the distance, not far from here, I can see another lift rising fast . . .'

*Extract from the address of K. L. Chun, Chairman of Chun Enterprises, at the UK launch of the Chun X-1 Personal Computer.*

1 Study the extract.

2 Present Chun's business philosophy in your own words.

1 Study the advertisement opposite.

2 List the main features of the X-1.

3 List its main competitive advantages.

74

# Announcing the Chun X-1 Personal Computer
# Personal Computing at less than £500 !

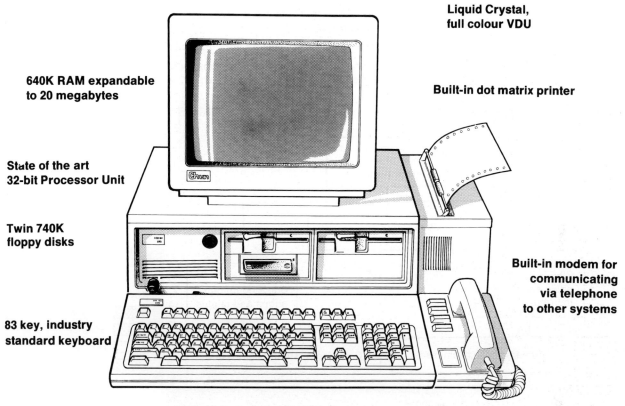

**Liquid Crystal, full colour VDU**

**640K RAM expandable to 20 megabytes**

**Built-in dot matrix printer**

**State of the art 32-bit Processor Unit**

**Twin 740K floppy disks**

**Built-in modem for communicating via telephone to other systems**

**83 key, industry standard keyboard**

**The £1000 computer package for less than £500**
**List price ex VAT £495**

When personal computer manufacturers tell you the price of their products they are usually telling you only half the story. They forget to tell you about those expensive peripherals that can double the price of the basic unit. The printer. The programs. The maintenance costs. Now, for the first time there is a personal computer whose price of under £500 tells you the whole story. It is called the Chun X-1 and it comes with a printer not only built into the price but into the computer itself. Add to this the free software package and the one year's free maintenance included in the price and we think you'll agree that the X-1 offers unbeatable value.

Ring 01-006-2111 for the whole story.

# Chun: quality and power... with economy built-in

# Overheard at the bar of the Markham Hotel

After the formal launch of the X-1, a few of Chun's UK dealers gathered in the bar of the hotel before the next session. Their initial enthusiasm and excitement had subsided a little. It wasn't what Chun had said that worried them. It was what he hadn't said.

1 Listen to some of the dealers talking.
2 What is their main concern?
3 List the reasons why they should become exclusive dealers for the X-1.

1 Study the handouts that the dealers received during the next session of the conference.
2 Describe Chun's present dealership structure.
3 Describe the major sectors of the home computer market and the changes expected in the next 3 years.

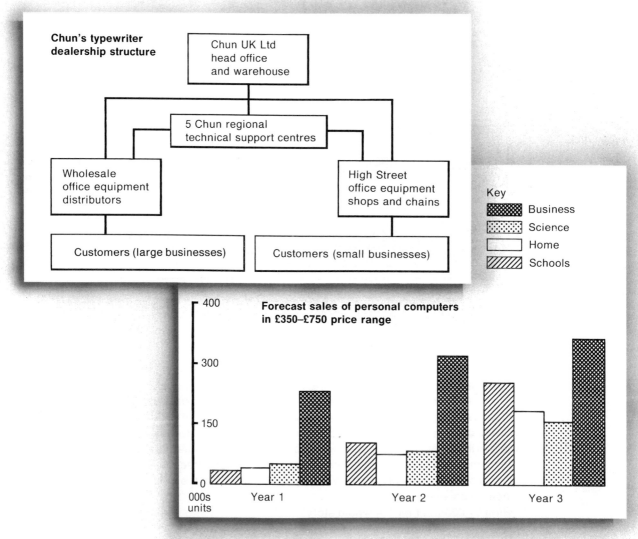

**Chun's typewriter dealership structure**

Chun UK Ltd head office and warehouse

5 Chun regional technical support centres

Wholesale office equipment distributors

High Street office equipment shops and chains

Customers (large businesses)

Customers (small businesses)

Key
- Business
- Science
- Home
- Schools

**Forecast sales of personal computers in £350–£750 price range**

400

300

150

0

000s units

Year 1    Year 2    Year 3

1 Listen to Chun summing up at the end of the first day of the conference.
2 Describe the 'deal' that he would like to do with his existing dealers.

# Burning the midnight oil

When Chun told his dealers to sleep on it, he knew that that was the last thing they would do. The lights of the Markham Hotel stayed on late that night. Small groups of dealers sat in corners discussing the pros and cons of different approaches to the new situation and, on the backs of cigarette packets and the corners of napkins, the outlines of various future distribution structures began to take shape.

1 Study the three possible structures below.

2 List some of the difficulties of selling to each of the 4 computer market sectors.

3 List some of the new skills that Chun's existing dealers will need to acquire to sell computers.

4 On the basis of the above decide which structure would be most suitable
   a) for Chun,
   b) for his dealers.

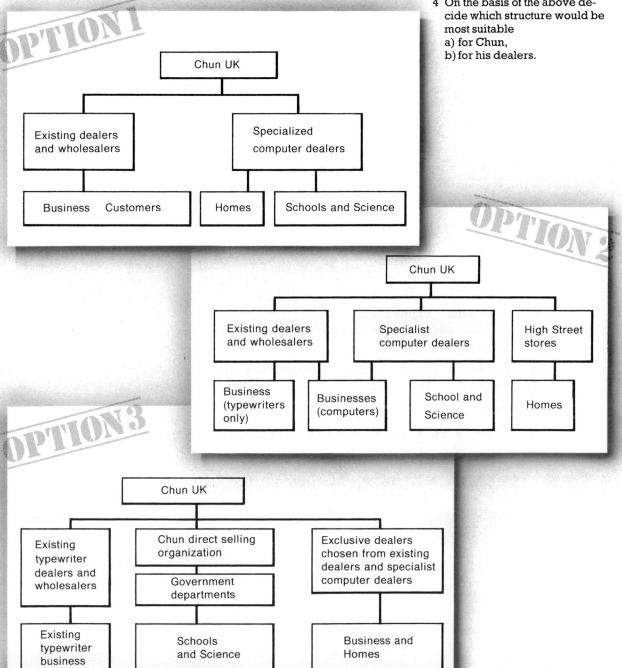

# The future begins here!

The next morning, after the opening session of the conference, the participants were asked to divide into small groups and each group was allocated a seminar room. In each room a member of Chun's management team waited to hear and discuss the proposals put forward by the dealers. Their brief was to come to an initial agreement about the future sales structure for the X-1 computer.

1 Divide into two groups
   a) The Chun management team,
   b) Chun typewriter dealers.

2 Using the agenda below, the Chun team should call a meeting and chair it.

3 The Chun dealers should present proposals with a view to winning the X-1 dealerships.

4 Both sides should sketch out an agreement for the future.

# Chun

AGENDA

1  Existing dealer expertise.

2  Requirements for future outlets for the X-1:

   a) Product expertise
   b) Knowledge and experience of market sector needs
   c) Technical support

3  Degree of advertising and promotion support needed for specialist sectors.

4  Training for dealers.

5  Sales targets and discounts. Period of contracts.

6  Escape clauses. Exclusivity clauses.

**REPORT**

1 Write a proposal to Chun UK Ltd outlining the ways in which you will adapt your present typewriter dealership to sell the new Chun Personal Computer.

2 Write a proposal to K. L. Chun himself recommending an overall structure of Chun's UK business to take account of the new product and the new market.

# Tapescripts

## Unit 1 Airline

**Page 1** InterAir's recorded information service

Hi, this is InterAir information with a recorded message for travelers on the Montreal-Toronto route. There are four kinds of ticket available. Business class is $130 round-trip. There are no restrictions for this class and your seat is guaranteed at any time. Economy class is $70 round-trip. The minimum reservation period is three weeks in advance and no changes to the reservation are allowed. The Advanced Economy fare is $55 round-trip. To qualify for this ticket, a reservation has to be made at least three months in advance and, again, no changes to the reservation are permitted. The Standby fare is $20 one-way. No reservations can be taken for this ticket and seats are allocated on a first-come first-serve basis subject to availability on individual flights. Flights from Toronto to Montreal leave at . . .

**Page 2** The conversation overheard at Toronto Airport

**Stevens** Morning, Pierre. Good trip?

**Malraux** Are you kidding? No, it was not. It never is these days.

**Stevens** O.K. O.K. I only asked.

**Malraux** I'm sorry, John. I've just about had enough. Our company pays $130 once a week to get me from Montreal to Toronto and back. For that price, I have to stand in line with screaming children, long haired students and terrified grandmothers asking me where the nearest toilet is . . .

**Stevens** But surely you fly Business Class?

**Malraux** That doesn't mean anything these days. Sure, I can get a seat whenever I want one. But for that privilege I have to pay $60 more than everyone else, I have to fight my way to my seat, climb over whole families to get it and then, when I get there, I find my backside doesn't fit into the thing!

**Stevens** Sounds most uncomfortable, Pierre.

**Malraux** Uncomfortable? Our parcels get better treatment on the railroad.

**Stevens** Well?

**Malraux** Well what?

**Stevens** What about the train?

**Malraux** It takes longer, doesn't it?

**Stevens** Not much. About an hour, I think. But it's all first class, plenty of room, desks, telephones . . .

**Malraux** Hm . . . I hadn't really considered it . . .

**Stevens** What do we do when we don't get value from our suppliers?

**Malraux** Ha. You're right, John. Complain.

**Stevens** Exactly. Don't tell *me* about your troubles. Tell the airline!

## Unit 2 Safety first

**Page 7** Harry Evans interviews some of the injured employees.

*First interview*

**Harry** So, what happened to you?

**First man** Oh, nothing much. I cut my thumb on a saw.

**Harry** How did it happen?

**First man** I'm not absolutely sure. One minute I was feeding a plank into the saw and suddenly it happened! Luckily, the guard was on, otherwise I'd have lost my thumb.

**Harry** Even so, your thumb did go under the guard?

**First man** Only a fraction, but there's got to be space for the wood to go in!

**Harry** Were you watching what you were doing?

**First man** 'Course I was! At least, I think I was.

**Harry** What time did it happen?

**First man** Just before the morning tea break.

**Harry** Do you think that had anything to do with it?

**First man** No! Mind you, it's a pretty long shift, that first one . . .

**Harry** So you, you could have been tired?

**First man** More likely looking at my watch! Shorter breaks, more often – that's what I say!

*Second interview*

**Harry** You say that a brick hit you on the back of the head?

**Second man** They say that's what happened. I never knew a thing about it.

**Harry** Were you wearing a helmet?

**Second man** No. It was just after the afternoon tea break. I hadn't put it back on.

**Harry** Why not?

**Second man** Well, I don't know. It was a nice day and I'd just been talking to my mates about . . . Anyway, after I just forgot to put it back on.

**Harry** But you knew about the danger?

**Second man** I've been working on sites like this for more than thirty years. Somehow, you just don't think it'll ever happen to you . . .

**Harry** So what do you think about helmets now?

**Second man** Ha! I'd go to bed in one if my wife'd let me!

*Third interview*

**Harry** How did you break your arm?

**Third man** I was working with the mechanical hoist. I'd just put in a batch of bricks when one got stuck. I put my hand in to free it when suddenly the hoist went up.

**Harry** Sounds very nasty.

**Third man** It wasn't pleasant. I was in hospital for a week.

**Harry** Does this machine break down often?

**Third man** Quite a lot. I'll tell you what's really wrong: the maintenance people work the same shifts as us. Really, they should be working when we're off. My accident happened just after lunch. See what I mean?

**Harry** Even so, aren't there procedures to follow when machines break down?

**Third man** Yeah. I should've turned the machine off and reloaded the bricks.

**Harry** But you decided to take a short cut?

**Third man** Come on! If we followed every damn procedure in the book, we'd never finish a job.

**Harry** But nor would you break your arm.

**Third man** Don't worry. I won't do it again.

## Unit 3 A tale of two Everests

**Page 9** The account of the climb

Great Achievements of the Twentieth Century
This week Paul Harper looks at the climbing of the south-west face of Everest in 1975.

Narrator: Mount Everest has captured the imagination of the world for centuries. It has challenged mountaineers to conquer its peak simply, as one climber once said, 'because it is there'. The mountain was first conquered in 1953. Since then, many have succeeded in reaching its summit and many have failed. It was in 1975, however, that a team of highly professional mountaineers decided to tackle the mountain by the most difficult route of all: the south-west face.

The south-west face of Everest presents special problems to climbers. It is the steepest and most exposed face of the mountain and has many obstacles, the most notorious of which is the rock band at 27,000 feet. For most climbers, this was a good reason for avoiding this route. For Chris Bonington and his team of 18 climbers, however, it represented one of the last great challenges in mountaineering.

Bonington is a modest and quiet man. He is also very thorough and knows that grand strategies will not work unless you take care of the details also. The first stage of the climb therefore began one year before the team arrived in Nepal. Finance was the key to it all. Sponsors had to be found to provide all the resources that the team would need. The team had to move fast and efficiently to take advantage of the short annual *weather window*. The first resource was therefore a computer to plan the logistics of moving 25 tons of equipment up the mountain without any of the supply bottlenecks that had defeated previous expeditions. The most important resource, however, was the team itself. It consisted of over 500 people of different cultures, personalities, skills and languages. Each had their place and it was the leader's function to weld them into one. Analytical people had to work with creative people. Individualists had to work within groups. It was clear from the start that only firm but sensitive leadership could achieve this.

Recruitment, then, was important. But, after this, a period of familiarization and acclimatization was essential. The second stage of the climb took care of this. During the approach march, Bonington delegated the organization and payment of the sherpas to their own cooperative. He also appointed a very young sherpa, Ptemba, to lead his people. This worked well. The Nepalese respected the decision and, when Bonington visited the Head Lama at Tangbotje Monastery to pay his respects, the relationship between Bonington and his porters and sherpas was cemented. As far as his own countrymen were concerned, Bonington involved himself in all the details of the operation, but also

allowed the team to criticize his ideas. With so many ambitious individuals, tension was never far from the surface. This was particularly true with respect to role allocation. Bonington decided not to select the lead team until much later in the climb. To do so at this stage would have demotivated some and encouraged others to become *prima donnas*.

The third stage of the climb was the establishment of Base Camp. In this stage Bonington had to allocate tasks. As expected, this caused friction and he admits there was the beginning of a shop floor mentality. However, as everyone was given responsibilities, this began to disappear. As Bonington said, he was like an admiral. He had to think of strategy all the time but had to be careful not to interfere in the tactical decisions of the ships' captains. Just above Base Camp, the team entered the first danger zone. The ice fall was where many deaths on earlier expeditions had occurred. The team made sure that the sherpas could see that they were taking all precautions. They also held a little ceremony at a shrine commemorating those who had died.

By the time the climbers reached Camp 4, the final decisions about the lead team had to be made. Bonington decided early on that he could not be in that team. He realized that his proper role was to coordinate the effort and to lead from behind. When the lead team was selected, there were few problems. By now, the team respected him and trusted each other. It had become a complete team effort.

The last major obstacle before the final assault was the rock band. A very experienced two man team was sent out to find a way through and, after some very tense hours, they returned with good news. The way was open for the final climb.

The last stage of the climb was prepared in great detail. The plan was to send out one team to prepare the route and then to have the lead team take over and make the final attempt on the summit. Reserve teams were to follow them. But, as often happens in such cases, things did not go to plan. As Bonington watched the first team through binoculars, it became clear that they were not turning back as planned. They had seen an opportunity and they were going for it, in spite of everything. Bonington admits that the tension was unbearable. But, when the radio message was received that the team had reached the peak, there was great joy amongst their team mates. The whole team had achieved their goal. It was a moment of totally shared satisfaction.

There is a postscript to this story, however. The reserve teams were also keen to have their chance. Bonington knew the weather was closing in, but he understood their need and let them go. Two more men reached the peak. Two others tried. One never came back. Everest had claimed one more life during the very moment of triumph.

**Page 11** Boswell's plan

*Stage 1* Boswell talks about the reorganization of the company and the design of the new pump.

**Boswell** . . . company shake-ups are always painful. But not half as painful as company failures.

**Interviewer** Mm . . . what exactly did the reorganization involve?

**Boswell** Well, there were two main aspects to it. Firstly, I had to get the supply side right. Now, that meant financial restructuring, considerable demanning and major investment in new plant and equipment. Secondly, I had to tackle the market problems. Well, Everest was trapped in a declining UK market and I had to change that fast.

**Interviewer** You mean exports?

**Boswell** Yes. At that time the Middle East was expanding fast. With the right product I knew we could get in there in a big way.

**Interviewer** From what you're saying, the reorganization was more like an earthquake than a shake-up.

**Boswell** Well, there was no alternative. The company needed firm management and clear, bold targets. It got both. As from that time on everyone knew exactly where they stood. If they didn't deliver, they were out. Now, as regards targets, I wanted a new heavy duty pump that could withstand the worst Sahara sandstorm and I wanted to sell 200,000 units of the new product by the end of year two. So what I did was this . . .

*Stage 2* Boswell talks about the production and testing of prototypes.

**Interviewer** The new pump was obviously the key to your plans. How did you go about designing it?

**Boswell** Well, I recruited six top designers, gave them their targets and told them to get on with it. It was a mistake. They couldn't agree on anything. In the end I had to go down there and impose a compromise.

**Interviewer** How did they react?

**Boswell** Two of them resigned on the spot. The rest carried on for a while until we reached the prototype stage. And that's when the bickering really started.

**Interviewer** What happened?

**Boswell** The prototype broke down during the dust tests. It was a diaphragm problem. All right. O.K., you always get teething troubles, that's what prototypes are for. But, when they blamed me because of the compromise solution, well, that's when I blew my top. Two more walked out. I had to bring in an outside consultant. We eventually got a working prototype but we were already three months behind schedule. . .

*Stage 3* Boswell talks about market testing and tooling up for full scale production.

**Interviewer** How long did it take to reach the production stage?

**Boswell** Wait a minute. I haven't told you yet what was happening on the shop-floor. While I was concentrating on the design problems, I left the reorganization of the shop floor to the personnel manager. Now, that's what personnel managers are for, isn't it? Anyway, out of the blue I get this delegation of machinists. They wanted me to remove one of the foremen. Said he was insulting them – you know the kind of thing. Anyway, I sent them back and carpeted both the foreman and the personnel manager. I am constantly amazed how often I have to remind people that business is about achieving targets and not about the colour of a bloke's skin.

**Interviewer** How did they react?

**Boswell** I didn't give them a chance to react. I simply told them that any racist comments would mean dismissal.

**Interviewer** Did that solve the problem?

**Boswell** Well, there were no more delegations.

**Interviewer** So production could go ahead.

**Boswell** First, we did a pre-production run. The problem there, however, was a 45% failure rate at quality control. We couldn't understand it at first. Then I got the work study man to look at systems and he discovered that half the machinists didn't understand the instructions from the supervisors. Now, sure they nodded. But the plain fact was they didn't speak English well enough.

**Interviewer** What action did you take?

**Boswell** Well, I sacked the personnel manager and started evening classes.

*Stage 4* Boswell talks about the start of full-scale production and the launch of the new product.

**Boswell** Of course, the quality control problem put us another three weeks behind schedule. Well, eventually we started production and the launch went ahead successfully. My team of four sales people were already in the Middle East looking for the crucial major order. I heard nothing for about three weeks, then one man came back with exhaustion and another resigned to take up another job. The other two did make progress. They both came up with the lead on a major ministry contract. The trouble was they started squabbling. I sorted that out by transferring one of them to another territory. And that left Chris Fawcett, an excellent salesman, to follow through. I gave him strict instructions to report every development to me. I didn't want any more foul-ups on the big one.

**Interviewer** And, in the meantime, you were building up stocks of the new pump?

**Boswell** Ha! Someone once said that business is about problem solving. Whoever it was, I agree with them. There was a hitch every step of the way. In this case, a bloke cut off a finger in a machine and they all demanded extra guards. Well, that cost money and it took two weeks before we came up with a compromise. And then, after all that, they went on strike!

**Interviewer** About safety?

**Boswell** Oh good heavens, no. They wanted an hour off for a holy day! After we'd already lost a fortnight's production! I ask you!

*Stage 5* Boswell talks about the sales breakthrough in the Middle East.

**Interviewer** Tell me about the final breakthrough.

**Boswell** Well, Fawcett finally got into direct negotiations with the Ministry and things seemed to be going well. It's my firm belief that in business everything depends on personal relationships. I decided therefore to fly out myself. The only thing left to haggle about was price and I wanted to be there when it was discussed. Well, we got to our bottom line and I stuck. There was the usual bluffing going on and I left Fawcett to sort out the details. After all, he understood the Arabs. At least, I thought he did.

*Stage 6* Boswell talks about the final stage of the negotiations.

**Boswell** I heard nothing for about a week after I got home. Then I had Fawcett on the phone sounding very de-

81

pressed. The Ministry had gone cold, he said. It was the price. OK, I said, we'll go down another 2% but that must be it. And I had to go abroad the next day and, apparently, Fawcett rang to ask for another 1%. We got that close! For God's sake, it was staring him in the face. He should have signed the deal and risked my anger. But no. We lost it. All for a lousy 1%.

## Unit 4 New Formula Miracle

**Page 15** James Toft describes the launch programme.

**Toft** Before I bring you up to date on the market figures, let me just recap on our marketing and launch strategy. First of all, we have never tested a product as thoroughly as we have tested New Formula Miracle. Not only did we test it exhaustively in the lab, we also trialled it in 5,000 households around the country. Out of that sample there was a 97% positive response rate. Only 3% reacted negatively. On the basis of these results, the launch decision was agreed and we brought in our advertising consultants. For reasons you are familiar with, their advice was to play down the enzyme content of Miracle and refer to it only as 'with Bioboost'. I think they were right.

The success of the launch seems to confirm this advice and we have had no negative responses from either retailers or consumers. In fact, we have the opposite. The £2m trade press advertising campaign brought in massive advance orders. The £8m TV and press campaign is now moving the new product from the shelves faster than we can get it out to the shops. We'll be following this with a door-to-door leaflet campaign at the end of November.

OK. Let me now give you the latest figures. Our first consumer audit shows we shifted £2.8m worth of New Formula Miracle in the first ten days and that, on my calculations, has given us 42% of the market which is already 2% above our original end-of-year targets. For this reason, I am recommending a revised end-of-year target of 50%. By the end of the year, there won't be a housewife in Britain who has not heard of New Formula Miracle. I have no doubt, ladies and gentlemen, that we have a winner on our hands.

**Page 17** The discussion of the crisis

**Sherrin** Look. All I'm saying is that it's very difficult, as you know, to avoid press attention when it's a human interest story that reaches into every home. Everyone uses washing powder and it gives them a thrill to think that they may become part of the news.
**Grant** Yeah, sure. I understand that. But did you give them the results of our lab tests and the consumer tests?
**Sherrin** But of course. At least, your version of them.
**Grant** And?
**Sherrin** Well, by that time the consumer groups and environmentalists had got onto it and only an independent scientific test would convince them. I was all for publishing our full lab results if you remember.
**Grant** That would've been suicide.

**Sherrin** Just because a 1% sample showed minor skin responses?
**Grant** Yes. The consumer groups and television have a wonderful way of finding that one person in a hundred and proving that the other ninety-nine are living in mortal danger!
**Sherrin** Well, even without our results, that is exactly what they have done. Two television consumer programmes devoted time to it and I appeared on one of them, if you remember. And numerous newspaper articles have dealt with it in one way or another.
**Toft** Now, just a minute, Diane. There is one question we haven't answered yet. *Is* there actually anything wrong with the new Miracle?
**Sherrin** I think the simple answer is 'no'. No more than any other washing powder containing enzymes.
Toft Then why has the housewife picked on us?
**Sherrin** Because we're the biggest and we made a lot of noise during the launch of Miracle.
**Grant** There was one housewife on that programme you mentioned, Diane, who impressed me. She said she felt betrayed. Do you remember? She had used original Miracle for years because it was soft and gentle to the skin. Then we launched New Formula and said nothing about enzymes. Her kids got rashes and now she's angry.
Toft And so is the National Skin Council and half the housewives of Britain. Come on! We know all this. The big question now is how we're going to get them all back on our side.

## Unit 6 Adventure Holidays International

**Page 26** The radio advertisement

Are you the kind of holidaymaker who expects to find the comforts of home only a hundred metres from your beach? Or the night life of a big city just a short ride from your hotel room overlooking the sea? If you are, then our adventure holidays are not for you.

At AHI we specialize in unusual holidays for unusual people. The kind of people who come on our holidays are the kind of people who don't like the word 'holiday'. They prefer the word 'experience'. Take, for example, our Caesar Itinerary through Northern Italy. Here you will travel on horseback in the company of Julius himself. You will cross the Rubicon river and march on Rome, staying overnight in ancient Italian villages. You will eat, drink, fight – yes, and play – as the Romans did. And, when you arrive at the Baths of Caligula in Rome, you will discover for yourself in five nights and days of celebration why Rome rose . . . and fell!

Call us on Freefone 3636. We have a range of experiences to choose from. Isobel in Spain, Alexander in Turkey and our most famous itinerary of all, Saladdin in Afaria.

Adventure Holidays International. Give us a ring. We dare you!

## Unit 7 Yamacom

**Page 31** The conversation between Paul Mackowitz and Hiroshi Watanabe

**Mackowitz** OK, Hiroshi, what's gone wrong this time?

**Watanabe** You tell me. You said you wanted a meeting.

**Mackowitz** All right. Let's go through it again. Two weeks ago we had a strong lead on the Marahito contract for the new Head Office. I asked for someone from your team to get in there quick and report back as fast as possible. What's happened? Nothing! Absolutely nothing!

**Watanabe** Not quite, Mr Mackowitz. You sacked Mr Shigeta.

**Mackowitz** Of course I did, Hiroshi. He refused to follow the reporting procedure. I never got one written contact report from him.

**Watanabe** He was one of our best salesmen.

**Mackowitz** I know that! But if you got targets, then you gotta have systems and procedures for achieving them. We need some energy in this organization, some zap! What's the matter, Hiroshi? Come on!

**Watanabe** We never had reporting systems in Yamahata. They are not necessary. Every salesman knows his client. Shigeta knows Marahito already. Things were going well there.

**Mackowitz** Then why didn't Shigeta tell me, for God's sakes?

**Watanabe** He did not want to displease you, Mr Mackowitz.

**Mackowitz** Displease me? All I wanted to know was what was happening!

**Watanabe** Mmm.

**Mackowitz** And, besides, Shigeta wasted time. Mine in particular. Every day he was over here waiting outside the office wanting to discuss this and that. I told him . . . For God's sake, use the phone, Katsushi. It's more efficient, reduces hassle. But no! Every day Katsushi sitting on my doorstep.

**Watanabe** He was worried about the advertising.

**Mackowitz** Oh, was he? And what's wrong with the advertising?

**Watanabe** He thought it was too strong. The Japanese like music, sky, pretty girls. Not too many strong voices.

**Mackowitz** Well, it works in every other damned market. Anyway, we're not here to talk about Shigeta. I want to know what's happening about the Marahito contracts. My God, Hiroshi, it's like trying to get blood out of a stone. Come on, now, what's happening?

**Page 31** The expert answers questions at the seminar on cross-cultural problems.

**Woman** . . . but the differences you've described, Mr Ichikawa, are so great that I don't see how we can bridge them.

**Expert** People of different cultures have always managed to bridge the gaps, sometimes very successfully. The first precondition for success, though, is mutual respect, the second is sensitivity and the third is – how shall I put it? – understanding the ways of the culture with which you are dealing.

**Woman** But surely the typical business person has got more important things to worry about than questions of culture? We're business people after all, not sociologists.

**Expert** If I may say so, that's a very Western way of looking at it. You take responsibility for one bit of life and let other people take care of the other bits. For you, it's all chopped up; for us, it's all one big whole.

**Man** And that's why we find it so difficult when we come to Japan. The lines of decision making are so unclear, it's all so . . . organic. I mean, it would really help if you could give us some real tips, Mr Ichikawa.

**Expert** Well, my first tip is to be patient. Everything takes much longer in Japan. For example, negotiations: I reckon it takes six times longer to complete a deal in Japan than in the U.S. You see, the Japanese like to get to know you first. They put a high value on personal relationships and they want to make sure that their potential partners are honest and sincere.

**Man** Sure. But what are the signals that tell us if things are going well or going wrong?

**Expert** There are lots of little things. In Japan it's the small gestures that count, not the big things.

**Man** For example?

**Expert** Gifts. These are valued for sentiment rather than actual value. They are very important. The whole business of entertainment is crucial. Don't be in a hurry. And another thing: don't be afraid of silence.

**Man** Pardon me?

**Expert** In Japan, silence is not a reason for embarrassment. It is not a negative signal as in your country. You'd be amazed how many unnecessary concessions have been made by Western business people just to keep the conversation going.

## Unit 8 Oxfam

**Page 37** The news that shocked the world

**Announcer** Here is the 10 o'clock news for Friday October 25. The latest reports from Ethiopia suggest that the famine situation there has now become critical. Latest estimates put the number of dead at over 10,000. In the last hour we have received this report from our correspondent in Ethiopia, Michael Bailey.

**Bailey** The situation here is desperate. I am speaking from one of Oxfam's feeding centres in Wollo Province. Normally about 1,000 people live in this area. There are now over 50,000 people in this camp alone. The land around me is dry, barren and exhausted. It has not rained properly for three years. There was a freak storm six weeks ago but all that did was to destroy the remaining crops. People are still arriving at the camp. Some of them have walked for weeks. When they arrive, the Oxfam staff identify the worst cases, usually children, pregnant women and the old, and they are taken immediately into the feeding centre for special treatment. The rest wait outside. Oxfam's Field Director here says that food, shelter, water and medical staff are needed immediately. The Organization, he says, has never faced a disaster of this scale before.

**Page 38** The emergency unit meets.

**Coordinator** OK, John, can you brief us on the likely food needs at the feeding centres?

**John** Yeah, but first of all, let's get one thing straight.

83

People who are severely malnourished can't digest normal foods. They'll need very special diets.

**Coordinator** Yes, Judith will talk about nutrition in a moment. What about the people who can eat grain?

**John** Well, we can buy the stuff on the open market at £115 per metric ton.

**Coordinator** And how far will one ton go?

**John** An adult needs 500 grammes per day. That means a ton will feed 33 people for 60 days.

**Coordinator** So we've got to work out how many tons we are going to need.

**Coordinator** Right then. Um, Judith, can we come on to the question of nutrition.

**Judith** Well, as John implied, grain will kill the severely malnourished. People need energy to digest food and grain would use up their last reserves.

**Coordinator** So?

**Judith** So we have to put the worst cases on special diets of powdered milk and Oxfam energy biscuits. Let's start with the biscuit. Basically, its high calorie content provides the energy needed just to keep the person alive. It's a vital stop-gap measure to keep people alive until better foods can arrive.

**Coordinator** How much do they need?

**Judith** Well, four biscuits a day as a supplement to their diet.

**Coordinator** Cost?

**Judith** Er . . . £1,300 per metric ton. And one ton will feed 160 children for 60 days.

**Coordinator** You say it's only a supplement?

**Judith** Oh, yes. The major part of the diet would be powdered milk and that's got protein for body building . . . let me see . . . yeah. That comes out at £588 per metric ton and that will feed 100 people for 60 days.

**Coordinator** Judith, these special diets, that's a specialist function, right?

**Judith** Yeah. I was coming on to that. We'll need nurse-nutritionists to administer the diets – our standard costing there is £9,000 per nurse – and I reckon we'll need 1 per 1,000 patients.

**Coordinator** Really?

**Judith** And that's assuming we have the transport to move them from centre to centre. And I reckon we'll need three Land-Rovers at £10,000 a piece.

**Coordinator** Right, Tony. Over to you now. What about shelter?

**Tony** Well, shelter is closely connected to the food situation. And vital energy is lost if people are cold, so we need clothing and blankets to keep people warm at night. Don't forget the temperature can go down to two degrees centigrade.

**Coordinator** So what's our target here?

**Tony** We're aiming to provide everyone with a blanket. We can get them for £3.15 each.

**Coordinator** And clothing?

**Tony** Well, the 'Knit for Africa' campaign is going well. We've got stocks of about 5,000 items at the moment so the only cost we'll incur there is transport to Addis.

**Coordinator** I see. What about tents?

**Tony** Far too costly. What I suggest is plastic sheeting for temporary shelter. It can be very effective and costs £55 per roll.

**Coordinator** How many people will that cover?

**Tony** I reckon about 14 average families, say 40 people.

## Unit 9 A severe case of TSV

**Page 43** The conversation between Max Smith and Pamela Bridges

**Bridges** Come in, Max. Do take a seat. Now . . .

**Smith** I suppose it's about the shift problem.

**Bridges** Well, that's one thing. But I wanted to have a chat about things in general, Max.

**Smith** I'd rather stick to specifics if you don't mind, Mrs Bridges.

**Bridges** All right. Well, let's talk about the medical problem.

**Smith** Fine.

**Bridges** Look. Can I say immediately that I want to clear this thing up as soon as possible and, if it means redesigning the tools or changing the shift patterns, then I'm sure we can reach an agreement?

**Smith** It's a bit late for that, Mrs Bridges. My members have already suffered their injuries.

**Bridges** Be fair, Max. We did provide tools for the job and we were very flexible on the question of manual assembly. Can I also remind you that we had no complaints about the manual process until a year after it was introduced?

**Smith** It takes time for some conditions to develop, Mrs Bridges. If the tool had been right in the first place, none of this would have happened.

**Bridges** With respect, Max, the tool is perfectly adequate.

**Smith** Not if you see it in the context of the present piece rate system.

**Bridges** Oh, I see.

**Smith** I'm glad you do, Mrs Bridges, because there's a lot of bitterness on the shop floor at the moment. There's been no pay rise for two years now and my members have been forced to use their hands simply to maintain their take home pay. Now we're seeing the human cost of that situation.

**Bridges** Oh, I think that's a bit dramatic, Max. There's nothing to suggest that people suffer long-term effects.

**Smith** We won't know that for some time, will we, Mrs Bridges? Now, if you don't mind, I don't see any point in continuing this conversation.

**Bridges** On the contrary, Max, you're the key man in all this.

**Smith** Not any more, Mrs Bridges. This morning I handed everything over to the Legal Officer of the Union. I have no doubt you'll be hearing from them shortly. Now if you don't mind . . .

## Unit 11 Please Mr Banker

**Page 54** The conversation between John Lyle and Mark Hampshire

**Lyle** Mark Hampshire?

**Hampshire** Speaking.

**Lyle** Hello. My name's John Lyle. I'm chairman of Autotech, the car components company.

**Hampshire** Oh, yes. I know of your company, Mr Lyle. How can I help you?

**Lyle** Well, Mr Hampshire, you've been recommended to me by one of my associates in the industry. I believe you handled a share flotation for Autopart two years ago.

**Hampshire** We did, yes.

**Lyle** Well, I'd rather not say too much at this stage. Let me put it like this, we have a new product in the pipeline which will take Autotech into a much wider market than the one we've served until now. Basically, we're talking about expansion, Mr Hampshire. We have the ball. We need someone to finance the bat for a couple of years.

**Hampshire** I see. From what I know of your company, Mr Lyle, you serve top of the market, specialist car manufacturers. And reading between the lines, you now want to move into serving the mainstream manufacturers.

**Lyle** That, of course, is strictly confidential. But, yes, that sums it up.

**Hampshire** Well. I think we should arrange a meeting, Mr Lyle.

**Lyle** That'd be fine with me.

**Hampshire** We shall need some background information ahead of the meeting; of course. Perhaps you could let me have a letter outlining your plans and requirements.

**Lyle** Of course.

**Hampshire** And we shall also need to look at your balance sheet and profit and loss figures for the last three years.

**Lyle** No problem. I can also provide you with a cash flow forecast for the product over the next three years.

**Hampshire** Good. One last thing, Mr Lyle. We shall, of course, need to look closely at the product itself.

**Lyle** I shall arrange a full presentation for you immediately.

**Hampshire** Fine. Now, perhaps we can agree a date for the meeting.

## Unit 12 Agrichem International

**Page 58** The telephone call to Agrichem's head office

**Secretary** Latin American Division. Can I help you?

**Sanchez** Yes. I'd like to speak to the regional director for South America, please.

**Secretary** Who's calling, please?

**Sanchez** My name is Sanchez and I'm the Vice-President, South America, for Fruitas Internacionales.

**Secretary** One moment, Mr Sanchez. Hello, Mr Sanchez. Go ahead please.

**Mathison** Good morning, Mr Sanchez. Mathison speaking.

**Sanchez** Good morning, Mr Mathison. I am ringing about a supply problem we have in Ecuador.

**Mathison** I see. What's the problem?

**Sanchez** As you know, we are one of the largest banana growers in South America and we use your products in most of our locations. In fact, our insecticide operations are now standard on your Martox. That's the good news, Mr Mathison. The bad news is that we cannot get Martox in Ecuador. At least, not at the time we want it or in the quantities we want it.

**Mathison** I see. Have you spoken to our distributor in Quito, Dr Nunez?

**Sanchez** How can you speak to someone who hasn't been in Quito for the last six months?

**Mathison** I meant his organization actually, Biopharm S.A.

**Sanchez** Mr Mathison, my people have written, spoken, visited and even played golf with the people at Biopharm. But still we cannot get the Martox we need.

**Mathison** Look. Can you leave this with me for an hour, Mr Sanchez? What's, what's, your immediate requirement?

**Sanchez** 10,000 litres.

**Mathison** OK. I'll be back to you soon.

**Sanchez** Before you go, Mr Mathison, I hear from my contacts that Nunez is a very busy man. It's just a pity that he hasn't got more time for your business. That *would*, however, be difficult from the Amazon basin.

**Mathison** The Amazon basin?

**Sanchez** Oil, Mr Mathison. Nunez has two exploration wells in the jungle down there. I am surprised you didn't know.

**Mathison** Thank you, Mr Sanchez. I'll be back to you within the hour.

**Page 60** Mathison and Thompson's discussion

**Mathison** So what are we looking for, Bill? An experienced operator or a new boy with ideas and enthusiasm?

**Thompson** It's a tricky one, Robert. On paper Nunez was ideal. He had the distribution system, the capital, the connections plus a degree in agricultural science.

**Mathison** But, in a company where everything depends on one man, than that man's got to be committed to the product.

**Thompson** Well, it's always the same if you ask me. We've either got to choose one of the big distributors whose business works so well that you don't have to worry about individuals or you've got to find that rare person who's got everything to win and who will sweat blood for the product.

**Mathison** Hm . . . I don't think we could ever take on someone without some kind of track record, Bill.

**Thompson** OK. What I'm saying is that the track record may not be in agrochemicals.

**Mathison** But he'd have to have product knowledge.

**Thompson** I'd say energy, enthusiasm and business knowledge come first. We could always provide the product expertise from here.

**Mathison** And what about a distribution system?

**Thompson** That's essential. But again, it needn't be specifically in agrochemical distribution. No, what I'm saying, Robert, is that we've got to find someone who wants some adventure. Someone with a record of quick, successful growth who we could help to adapt if necessary to agrochemicals.

**Mathison** Well, there are lots of risks, Bill. It'd be much safer to give it to one of the established distributors.

**Thompson** Most of them already have links with our major competitors. There'd be a problem of conflict of interest. Also, we don't want someone who just wants to fill a gap in their present portfolio, who is trying to get out of a problem situation with its present product range. We don't want Martox to be just another insurance policy. We want it to be someone's life blood!

**Mathison** Bill, I'm beginning to think you have someone in mind already?

**Thompson** I know a lot of people out there. None of them are ideal. I have, however, come up with a short list. I think we should look through it together very carefully . . .

## Unit 13 Our man in Nam Doa

**Page 66** Berling calls the Ministry.

**Ban Dong** Hello.

**Berling** Hello?

**Ban Dong** Ah, Mr Berling. I was going to ring you. You have heard, then, about the trouble in Nam Doa?

**Berling** I have just heard, Mr Dong, and I'm trying to get to the bottom of it.

**Ban Dong** Let me try and fill you in then. The project is at a standstill because yet another of your men has gone absent. Apparently, he flew here on Sunday.

**Berling** Ah, yes, I know.

**Ban Dong** Have you spoken to him yet?

**Berling** No, not yet. I was trying to.

**Ban Dong** Then you don't know about a fight?

**Berling** What fight?

**Ban Dong** Mr Wikström hit one of our foremen. There was an argument about training. Apparently, Mr Wikström explained to our people what to do once and, then, if they could not do it, he did it himself. He made our people very angry. You see, training is part of the contract, Mr Berling. Our people expect it. You should also remember that our people do not always speak very good English.

**Berling** Can you give me some more details?

**Ban Dong** There is one other thing.

**Berling** What's that?

**Ban Dong** The problem of *Mrs* Wikström.

**Berling** But she's here in the capital.

**Ban Dong** Correction, Mr Berling. She went up to Nam Doa a week ago.

**Berling** What?

**Ban Dong** She was fed up waiting for accommodation to be found so she flew up to be near her husband and also because she felt she could do something to help the development of our country.

**Berling** Oh God.

**Ban Dong** She's staying at a police station.

**Berling** What do you mean, 'staying'?

**Ban Dong** She's still there. Apparently, she's running short language courses for our workers there.

**Berling** I'll fly up as soon as possible, Mr Dong. I'm very sorry about all this and . . .

**Ban Dong** Please don't interrupt the language lessons. I'm more interested in getting a replacement for *Mr* Wikström. The project is already six months behind schedule.

## Unit 15 Chun and the desktop computer

**Page 76** The dealers talking

**First dealer** Chun's playing his cards very close to his chest, Jack.

**Second dealer** Mm? I thought he was being very open.

**First dealer** Sure. On the technical side, he was. I'm talking about the sales side. He kept saying 'X-1 dealers will . . .' He wasn't talking to us, Jack! He was talking to people he had not met yet.

**Second dealer** Come off it! You're imagining things.

**First dealer** No. Just think about it for a moment. The X-1 is a totally new product to us. It's also aimed at markets that most of us are not connected with. Would you sell a computer through a typewriter dealer?

**Second dealer** For goodness sake, we made Chun in this country! Without us, there would be no Chun U.K.

**First dealer** So?

**Second dealer** So he owes it to us. There's such a thing as loyalty, Jack.

**First dealer** You can only be loyal if you are successful and that's what Chun will want first.

**Second dealer** But we are successful, Paul. You personally shifted 3,000 units last year.

**First dealer** Typewriters, my friend. Not personal computers. This is why he's being careful. There'll be no exclusivity clauses for us until Chun is convinced that we are the right people for the job.

**Page 76** Chun's summing-up

Chun: So, ladies and gentlemen, we are willing to listen. We have not made up our minds and we will not do this until we have discussed the situation with all of you. We want a fair deal for Chun and a fair deal for each of you. What is more, we are willing to invest a certain amount in you if you wish to become X-1 dealers. In return, however, we will want results across the whole personal computer market. Am I asking too much? That depends on what kind of proposals you can put forward tomorrow. Sleep on it, everyone. Tomorrow could be the first day of a bright new future for us all.